The RAISING of the 144,000

SCROLL 1
(ADEPT OCCULT SERIES)

Published 2022:
Golden Child Promotions Publishing Ltd
Portland House,
Belmont Business Park,
Durham,
DH1 1TW

onlygold@gcpp.gold

gcpp.gold

Copyright © 31st December, 2022 by Kwadw(o) Naya: Baa Ankh Em Re A'lyun Eil, Dr Leon Moss, Shawn Pereira, Cyrlene, Daniel Raine, and Akinsola Olayinka.

All rights reserved. No part of this publication may be reproduced, stored in a retrieval system or transmitted in any form or by any means, electronic, mechanical, photocopying, recording, and/or otherwise without prior written permission of the publishers. This book may not be lent, resold, hired out or otherwise disposed of by way of trade in any form, binding or cover other than that in which it is published, without the prior consent of the publishers.

HAVE YOU READ OMNI-U

You can get this book using the link below. Please do not delay:

https://BookHip.com/QHPBRT

ACKNOWL-EDGMENTS

Acknowledgment and thanks to Hayley, for the editing.

Thanks also to Hansbarrow Creatives for the formatting and book production.

Thanks to the 'good' brother Jose Olapade for the book cover design, it does shine.

Thanks to all the contributors from Pexels for assisting us with the illustrations.

A BIG WARM THANKS to **THE GOLDEN TEAM**; without them, this **DIVINE CREATION** would have **NEVER** been **BIRTHED** into **EXISTENCE**.

Let us not forget about all the other wonderful staff at Golden Child Promotions Publishing Ltd, especially Femi, the web developer (who painstakingly spends hours doing his work, most often unappreciated).

…But…

THE BIGGEST THANKS, ACKNOWLEDGMENTS, AND APPRECIATION MUST GO TO YOU.

For without **YOUR SUPPORT**, there would **BE NO POINT**.

DEDICATION

Dedication

This book is dedicated to **ALL** of the **TRUTH-SEEKERS** '**OUT THERE**'.

It is dedicated to **ALL** the people who wish to **WAKE-UP** and to those who are already **AWAKE!**

It is dedicated to the people who would rather use their **REAL EYES**.

To **STOP** them from getting **DECEIVED** by the **REAL LIES**.

It is dedicated to **ALL** who wish to **SEE** the '**THINGS**' as they **REALLY ARE**.

<u>**IS THIS YOU?**</u>

PREFACE

Preface

Many people come, but few are chosen!

WE have come to find the **LIVING** amongst the dead.

WE have come to find the **144,000** who wish to be **RAISED.**

You **KNOW WHO YOU ARE** or **WILL** once **YOUR DNA** has been **RE-ACTIVATED!**

NOW is the **TIME!**

COME AND JOIN US, my brothers and sisters.

THIS IS NOT ABOUT COLOR, CREED, OR RACE.

IT IS ABOUT RIGHTEOUSNESS, DIVINE LOVE, DIVINE TRUTH, DIVINE WISDOM, and **SERVICE** to **HUMANITY.**

The **TIME** for **DEBATING** has **GONE**, now is a **TIME** for **LOVING, LEARNING, SHARING, CARING, NURTURING, EVOLVING,** and **GROWING**.

NOW IS THE TIME FOR UNITY AND GROWTH - FOR EACH ONE TO TEACH ONE.

CURSED SEEDS ARE NOT WELCOME!

This is for the **CHOSEN ONES!**

Preface

THE GOLDEN ONES!

THE RIGHTEOUS ONES!

THE DIVINE!

OF THE HIGHEST EILOHEEM!

YOU KNOW WHO YOU ARE (If not, you wouldn't be here).

Question: Who are the **144,000?** Or is it 1 + 4 + 4 = 9?

The **ELEVATION** towards **OUR** highest sense and state of being?

(Isn't nine the highest number, after all?)

Answer: This is the wrong question to be asking, really, isn't it?

I will tell you why:

Many people have different interpretations of this, rightly so.

Preface

WE ALL SEE THINGS DIFFERENTLY, and **WE ALL** have different viewpoints, ideals, and perspectives backed up by different levels of innerstanding.

Who is to **SAY WHO IS RIGHT** and **WHO IS WRONG?**

WHO is **CAPABLE** of the **BALANCEMENT** and **JUDGEMENT** of these **THINGS?**

WE will happily show you what **WE SEE THROUGH OUR EYES!**

WE are the **ELECTED EILOHEEM** from **NATURE, LIGHTING** up this **TAPAL (WORLD)** with **OUR** positive powers and forces.

WE ALL HAVE THE KEY (ANKH).

Preface

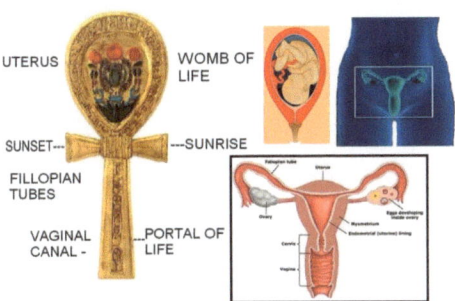

A-mun/Amunet

N-un/Nunet

K-ek/Kekhet

H-eh/Hehet

AND WE WILL ALL GIVE YOU (THE WORD) DIVINE TRUTH!

[1] Amunet, consort of Amun, Karnak Temple, Luxor, Egypt
1   https://www.flickr.com/photos/chrisjohnbeckett/5137565246/ accessed 18th August 2021 @ 22:56

Preface

² Colossal statue of Amunet erected by Tutankhamun in Karnak Temple, Luxor, Egypt

2   https://upload.wikimedia.org/wikipedia/commons/4/4c/AmonetKarnaKLuxor121.jpg Permission details: CC-BY-SA-2.5; Released under the GNU Free Documentation License accessed 18th August 2021 @ 22:56

Preface

³ Statues in Karnak and Luxor with the facial features of Tutankhamun and Ankhesenamen. On the left: Amun and Amunet in Karnak.

---
3   euler.slu.edu accessed 18th August 2021 @ 23:09

Preface

4 A History Upon the Sky - Fantastic Story

Many folks believe or think that this is only a mystery but is it a mystery, my story, or our story?

Whatever happened to **HIS-STORY?**

How do **YOU PERCEIVE** this **FANTASTIC STORY?**

We will talk about all this stuff a little later, but for now, let us proceed…

---

4   http://fantasticstory.weebly.com/uploads/2/1/9/8/21985000/3672413_orig.jpg accessed 18th August 2021 @ 23:28

CONTENTS

Contents

Acknowledgments v

Dedication vii

Preface ix

Introduction 01

Advancement 1: Divine Love 06

Advancement 2: God & The Devil 16

Advancement 3: God & The Devil 34

Advancement 4: Choose Your Master & Reap What You Sow 40

Advancement 5: Trials & Tribulations . 48

Advancement 6: Integrity 80

Advancement 7: Imagination & Creativity 104

Advancement 8: Who Is God & The Devil? 116

Advancement 9: The Rapture Is Here & Now! 120

Conclusion..**134**

Afterword **140**

About The Authors **146**

"There will be a group of 144,000 people who will form the foundation for a new society.

Someone has to LEAD THE WAY, right?" - The Golden Team

INTRODUCTION

Introduction

My name is Cyrlene. I left home at 12 years old and went through so many trials and tribulations, where I had reporters and magazines contact me for the stories.

Back then, you didn't chat about your business as such, even when money was offered to you. From a young age, my friends always told me that I should write a book, I didn't think this would happen, but here I am today and realize the importance of sharing your stories. There must be a reason I went through what I did, and I'm sure it wasn't to keep it to myself. Now I am ready to go with no fear, no shame, because one thing is for sure, I will not go to my grave with all these terrible truths. I feel I am here to share what I've been through, to inspire, encourage and give strength to some of you who are struggling to come to terms with life's teachings, and to know that you can overcome anything and still be a success in life.

I was startled when I was asked to do the intro to this book; nevertheless, I agreed.

This book has both established and renowned authors, as well as 3 new authors. It is a pleasure and very encouraging that the more experienced authors who have already published some brilliant works and are happy to produce work along with us newbies.

Introduction

A book where the authors are from across the continents i.e. Nigeria, USA, and the UK, with established writers that have some serious knowledge, and already published some brilliant work and agreed to be part of this project with three of us that are putting out our first pieces of work. This is so inspiring.

What stood out for me is that we all wrote our pieces without discussing what we were writing about, but it seems to all fit together and flow well. This book shows that we all have integrity, love, passion, morals, respect, insight into life, and something to offer to a wide range of people.

This book will give you true insight into our lives and will empower those that read it, and there will be further opportunities to connect with any author you have a synergy with.

This book is packed with **KNOWLEDGE** of the **HIGHEST ORDER.**

Hopefully, **YOU** will be able to **TAKE** from it.

YOU will probably want to **READ** it **TIME** and **TIME AGAIN** it is that good.

Don't just believe us.

Kindly **CHECK IT OUT FOR YOURSELF.**

Introduction

THANK YOU for **BEING** with **US TODAY.**

ENJOY 🤍 😀 🤍

ADVANCEMENT

DIVINE LOVE

Advancement 1: Divine Love

RAAHUBAAT- (Greetings).

DIVINE LOVE is **THE WAY, TRUTH,** and **LIGHT** of **THIS WORLD!**

Pure consciousness is the highest level of reality.

To reach it, **YOU MUST OVERSTAND**, merge in, and **BECOME DIVINE LOVE!**

WHAT is **DIVINE LOVE?**

DIVINE LOVE is **RECOGNITION** of **THE BREATH OF LIFE,** the **LIFE FORCE** that is **WITHIN ALL!**

Not just **KNOWING** this **INTELLECTUALLY** but having **TRUE AWARENESS** of it because it **WILL TRANSFORM YOU** into **DIVINE REALITY!**

LOVE is the **FORCE THAT WILL** cause **YOU** to shift **YOUR ATTENTION** to **DIVINE REALITY**.

Which **SYMBOLICALLY** is the opening of **YOUR CROWN CHAKRA.**

In our ancient language or one of our ancient languages, the word we use is **LAAHUT (ONENESS).**

ONENESS with **THE MOST HIGH**, which is **KULUWM**, which is **ALL!**

Without **AWARENESS** of **DIVINE LOVE, YOU WILL NEVER REACH IT!**

Most people's **IDEA** of **LOVE** is based on **CONDITIONS**.

The human **LOVES** like:

A **LOVE** for a **MATE**

Or the **LOVE** of a **CHILD**

Or **LOVE** for **WHAT YOU CAN DO FOR ME**

Or **I LOVE YOU** because **YOU MAKE ME FEEL**

All those **LOVES** are a part of it but are not the **HIGHEST FORMS** of **LOVE**!

The scriptures or the Christian bible says, "God is **LOVE**."

Now jealousy, when they interpret God being a jealous God in those scriptures, that is not **THE HIGHEST FORM** of **LOVE**!

So that could **NEVER** be **THE MOST HIGH**

because jealousy is a **HUMAN** flaw.

That is someone's **MISINTERPRETATION** of **GOD**!

I have heard **GOOD** people **SAY** that they **ACCEPT EVERYTHING** that **THE BIBLE SAYS WITHOUT QUESTION.**

And as **GOOD** as they are or appear to be, they **WILL NEVER** reach **DIVINE REALITY** in that **STATE** of **MIND.**

They are not humble enough to even **QUESTION** an **ATTRIBUTE** so **HORRENDOUS** or **FLAWED** as **JEALOUSY.**

THE SOURCE CAN NEVER BE JEALOUS OF ITS OWN SELF!

If its **ESSENCE** is **THE SOURCE OF LIFE** and that **SOURCE**

OF LIFE is within **ALL**, then **WHO** is there to be **JEALOUS** of?

There is **NO LIFE** and **NO LIGHT** and **NO EXISTENCE** without **THE LIFE FORCE!**

So, it's **ALL ONE**.

So, somebody is trying to intentionally (or, I will give you the benefit of the doubt), shall I say unintentionally, **DECEIVE US** by saying that we should worship a **JEALOUS** God.

It's **CLEAR** if **YOU STUDY** those scriptures **properly** that most of the descriptions of this God are based on and rooted in **HUMAN ATTRIBUTES**.

Is someone trying to under-**STAND THE CREATOR?**

YOU CAN NEVER really under-**STAND THE CREATOR**.

YOU have to **MERGE** with **THE CREATOR** to **OBTAIN** an **OVER**-standing.

As long as **YOU** are under-**STANDING, YOU** are beneath and not **ONE WITH!**

So, **LOVE** is **THE KEY.**

DIVINE LOVE!

Advancement 1: Divine Love

UNCONDITIONAL LOVE!

That means I don't have to like what **YOU** do, but I must **BOW** to the **DIVINITY** that is **WITHIN YOU.**

I MUST ACKNOWLEDGE WHO YOU ARE!

Even someone that would be considered **EVIL!**

The **EVILNESS EXISTS** because that **BEING** is not **AWARE** of it's own **SELF.**

It's **own ESSENCE** that is **WITHIN ALL!**

It's **SEES** it-**SELF** as **SEPARATE, BETTER,** or **WORSE.**

It **SEES** or **LIVES** in a **DUALITY FRAME** of **MIND.**

It's **CONFUSED** because of the **MANIFESTED REALITY,** meaning the **FORMS, THE SHAPES, THE PLACES, THE PEOPLE, THE THINGS.**

It is **BLINDED** by **THE LIGHT**!

LIGHTS!

CAMERAS!

ACTION!

It is **BLINDED** by **PRODUCTION**.

THE PRODUCTION is **THE PLAY** of **LIFE**.

The **REALITY** is that **THE PLAY** of **LIFE** is **PLAYED** by **THE ONE ESSENCE**, **THE SOURCE** who **MANIFESTS** in **ALL**!

SELFISHNESS is the **FLAW** of **HUMANITY**.

Some people say **SELFISHNESS**. **WE** can say **EGO**. **WE** can say **THE IDEA** that **YOU** are **SEPARATE** from **THE WHOLE** is **THE CAUSE** of **ALL TROUBLE**!

THE CAUSE of **ALL** **SUFFERING**.

KNOWING this **INTELLECTUALLY** is **NOT ENOUGH**!

YOU MUST DISCIPLINE YOURSELF THROUGH MEDITATION.

There is **NO SHORTCUT** on a **SPIRITUAL PATH**!

YOU MUST MEDITATE and **MEDITATE WITH DIRECTION** or with **INSTRUCTION**.

YOU MUST MEDITATE PROPERLY!

Not everyone **KNOWS** **HOW** to **MEDITATE PROPERLY**.

MEDITATION IS OBSERVATION!

It is not doing anything other than **OBSERVING** so that **YOU** can **REALIZE** with **YOUR REAL EYE, YOUR INNER EYE,** that **YOU** are **SEPARATE** from **YOUR BODY, YOUR THOUGHTS,** and **YOUR EMOTIONS.**

And the **YOU** that is **SEPARATE** is the same **YOU** that's in **ALL** and is **ALL.**

ALL is.

There is a **LEVEL** of **EXISTENCE** that's **OBSERVING ITS OWN CREATION. IT'S OWN MANIFESTATIONS.** It's **OBSERVING** it **NOT DOING ANYTHING!**

BUT YOU MUST BE STILL ENOUGH!

BE STILL and DISCOVER **I AM, THAT I AM!**

DISCOVER THE GREAT I AM!

THE GREAT I THAT EXISTS!

THE ONE I THAT EXISTS.

THE REAL YOU!

This is **OUR MESSAGE.**

It is not a **COMPLEX MESSAGE.**

It is not a **DEEP MESSAGE.**

THIS IS THE MESSAGE, THE WORD!

THAT HAS BEEN MADE FLESH!

AMONG or **AS YOU** 😊.

BECOME <u>THE WORD</u> BY WAY OF DISCOVERING <u>THE WORD</u> THAT IS YOU.

<u>**THE WORD**</u> is <u>**GOD**</u> and was <u>**GOD**</u>, meaning <u>**IS**</u> and <u>**WAS**</u> and <u>**WILL ALWAYS BE**</u> but also <u>**MANIFESTS IN FORM!**</u>

This is **THE BIGGEST SECRET,** that is **SACRED!**

And **THE SOLUTION** to **THE GLOBAL PROBLEMS HUMANITY FACE.**

The further **YOU** get **AWAY** from **THIS REALITY,** the **MORE CHAOS,** and that is what **WE** are **SEEING** in **THE WORLD – CHAOS.**

But there are groups of **US** who work to **PERFECT OURSELVES** so **WE** can **BE** the **ANGELOS – THE ANGELS.**

TO DELIVER THE MESSAGE.

THE WORD!

WADU

PEACE AND LOVE!

Dr. Leon Moss (Aka Hotep Tal Amun)

Feel free to visit my website, look around, check out the services, etc. We are always here to help:

https://www.drleonmoss.gold/

ADVANCEMENT

GOD & THE DEVIL

Advancement 2: God & The Devil

> *"Service to others is the rent we pay for our room here on earth."*
>
> – Muhammad Ali

Hi, its Kwadw(o). Some call me Baa. I hope you are all well!

I KNOW WHY I am here.

But I didn't really ever **THINK** or **ENVISAGE** so **PRIOR**.

I am not a **TEACHER**, doctor, or lawyer. I don't think that I would even be a good criminal, either.

But I am here.

My mother always used to say to me when I was younger – **"THOSE WHO KNOW BETTER SHOULD DO BETTER."**

I have had these words '**RINGING**' in my head all my **LIFE!**

THANKS, MOTHER!

I guess it is my **CALLING**.

It is both a pleasure and an honor to be involved in a book with other authors of such magnitude, in fact, my wildest dream.

I am deeply humbled and will try not to let everybody down.

What am I writing about?

Do I even know?

Let me take a **LOOK**…

GOD and the **DEVIL**.

Everybody knows who is **GOD** and **WHO** is the **DEVIL**, don't they?

They **ALL** have some **VERSION**, some **STORY**.

Advancement 2: God & The Devil

To me, **GOD** and the **DEVIL** are just two words.

Just like any other words;

Two words at different ends of the **POLARITY** scale.

One is at the **NORTH POLE**, and the other is at the **SOUTH POLE**, and sometimes they **SWITCH**.

Just kidding.

The **WORD 'GOD'** generally relates to **GOOD**.

It even **LOOKS LIKE GOOD** – can you not **SEE**?

The **WORD 'DEVIL'** relates to **LIVED** as in **PAST/EX-PIRED.**

The **WORD 'DEVIL'** also relates to **EVIL** – can **YOU SEE** that **ALSO**?

It is **ALL** in the **SPELL-ING!**

WORDS are very **IMPORTANT.**

WORD is **TRUTH.**

Be careful with the **WORDS YOU SPEAK** unless **YOU KNOW** the **MEANING.**

Unfortunately, so many of **US** do not have an **OVERSTANDING** or even **INNERSTAND.**

Most people can only under**STAND!**

They can only stand **UNDER** the **KNOWLEDGE.**

Always **STUCK** in **3D**. What strange geometrics.

Shouldn't we be working in the **5TH DIMENSION** by now, at the very least?

But most of **US** are **STILL GOVERNED** by **TICK TOCK.**

Not the mobile application.

Don't **YOU THINK** that it is **TIME** that **WE ALL** flip the **SCRIPT?**

CHANGED THE NARRATIVE?

LET US BREAK THE SPELL!

THE SUN IS COMING.

LET US KEEP SHINING.

People ask silly questions **ALL** the **TIME**, such as do **YOU BELIEVE** in **GOD** or the **DEVIL?**

SILLY, SILLY, SILLY.

Because if one **BELIEVES**, then they do not actually **KNOW**.

As Tony Robbins would say, "Belief is a poor substitute for **KNOWLEDGE**."

Next time you don't **KNOW** something, try not believing people. Try getting into the habit of finding the **DIVINE TRUTH** for **YOURSELF**.

It is always best.

To **KNOW** or **NOT** to **KNOW, THAT IS THE QUESTION.**

First, **WE** will get into the definitions.

Let **US LOOK** up the **ETYMOLOGY (ROOT)** and **DEFINITIONS** of both words. Let's **SEE** what **WE** find:

"First Known Use of God

Noun

before the 12th century, in the meaning defined at sense 1

Verb

1595, in the meaning defined above

History and Etymology for god

Noun and Verb

Middle English, from Old English; akin to Old High German got god." 5

As **WE** can **SEE** from the etymology, god was defined before the 12th century as a **NOUN**, which means that the word relates to a **PERSON**, **PLACE**, or **THING**.

Please correct me if I am wrong.

WE can **SEE** that the word 'god' relates to a **PERSON, PLACE, or THING,** *"defined at sense 1"*.

What is *"sense 1"*?

Let **US** take a **LOOK** at the definition.

"god

noun

\ 'gäd also 'gȯd \

plural gods

---

5 https://www.merriam-webster.com/dictionary/god Accessed 7th May 2020 @ 21:44

Definition of god'

(Entry 1 of 2)

1 God : the supreme or ultimate reality: such as

a : the Being perfect in power, wisdom, and goodness who is worshipped (as in Judaism, Christianity, Islam, and Hinduism) as creator and ruler of the universe Throughout the <u>patristic</u> and <u>medieval</u> periods, Christian theologians taught that God created the universe ...— Jame Schaefer ... the Supreme Being or God, the personal form of the Ultimate Reality, is conceived by Hindus as having various aspects.— Sunita Pant Bansal

b Christian Science : the incorporeal divine Principle ruling over all as **eternal Spirit : infinite Mind**

2 or less commonly God : a being or object that is worshipped as having more than natural attributes and powers specifically : one controlling a particular aspect or part of reality Greek gods of love and war

3 : a person or thing of supreme value had photos of baseball's gods pinned to his bedroom wall

Advancement 2: God & The Devil

4 : a powerful ruler Hollywood gods that control our movies' fates." [6]

As **WE** can **SEE**, the word 'god' has several definitions.

It doesn't stop there. Since 1595 the word 'god' was also used in a transitory sense, as you can see below:

"god

<u>*verb*</u>

godded; godding

Definition of god (Entry 2 of 2)

<u>*transitive verb*</u>

: to treat as a god : <u>idolize</u>, <u>deify</u>." 7

Which is not very cool. **WHY CHANGE** things for the **WORSE**?

Does that even make **SENSE?**

---

6   https://www.merriam-webster.com/dictionary/god Accessed 7th May 2020 @ 22:04

7   https://www.merriam-webster.com/dictionary/god Accessed 7th May 2020 @ 22:32

To some, maybe, it is **TIME** to **CHANGE** the **RHETORIC**. Don't **YOU THINK?**

As **WE** can surmise from **(BOTH)** the **ETYMOLOGY** and the **DEFINITION**, god means in a **ROOT SENSE "THE SUPREME** or **ULTIMATE REALITY."**

QUESTION: So, what is **GOD**?

ANSWER: <u>THE SUPREME</u> or **<u>ULTIMATE REALITY</u>** – (**<u>THE ALL</u>**).

Which, to me, makes perfect sense.

NEED WE SAY MORE?

What are **YOUR THOUGHTS?**

Let **US** move on to the word devil.

What does it mean?

"First Known Use of devil

Noun

before the 12th century, in the meaning defined at sense 1

Verb

1787, in the meaning defined at sense 1

History and Etymology for devil

Noun

Middle English devel, del, dule, going back to Old English dēofol, dīoful, going back to West Germanic *diuvul- (whence also Old Frisian diūvel, diōvel, Old Saxon diuḃal, Middle Dutch duvel, Old High German tiuval, tiufal), probably borrowed from an early Romance outcome of Late Latin diabolus "the Devil," borrowed from Greek diábolos (New Testament, Septuagint, as a rendering of Hebrew śāṭān satan), earlier, "accuser, backbiter, slanderer," agentive derivative of diabállein "to take across, put through, set at variance, attack (a person's character), accuse, slander," from dia- dia- + bállō, bállein "to reach by throwing, let fly, strike, put, place," going back to earlier *gʷəl-n-ō or *gʷəl-i̯-ō, perhaps going back to an Indo-European base *gʷelh₁-

Note: The standard English pronunciation of devil with the outcome of a short vowel presumably reflects shortening of the Old English dipththong -ēo-/-īo- in syncopated forms, as the nominative plural dēoflas. The early Modern English form divel (as in Shakespeare), preserved in regional and dialectal speech in both Britain and the U.S., shows Middle English shortening of original ẹ̄ to i.

Forms such as Middle English dele and early Scots dele show loss of v before a syllable ending in a liquid. — Greek bállein and its many prefixed forms are rich in nominal derivatives, usually with o-grade (as in diábolos, perhaps secondarily agentive, after the adjective diábolos "slanderous, backbiting") or with zero grade blē- (going back to *gʷlh₁-C-). That the original consonant was a labiovelar is assured by the Arcadian form esdellō, with e-grade, corresponding to Greek ekballō "expel, let fall." Despite its thoroughly Indo-European formal properties, bállein has no certain cognates outside Greek.

Verb

derivative of devil entry 1." [8]

Have you noticed the constant **CHANGES** in the English **TONGUE** from Olde English to modern English as **TIME** has gone by?

Oh, **WHY**, oh, **WHY**, oh, **WHY**?

As **WE** can **SEE** with the word 'devil,' things are not much different.

Maybe, opposite in polarity.

8   https://www.merriam-webster.com/dictionary/devil#synonyms
    Accessed 7th May 2020 @ 23:06

WE can see from the etymology devil/Devil before the 12th century was a **NOUN**, which means that the word relates to a **PERSON**, **PLACE**, or **THING**, just the same. Another **3-dimensional entity.**

Let **US** take a **LOOK** at the definition:

"devil

<u>noun</u>

dev·il | \ ˈde-vᵊl , dialectal ˈdi- \

Definition of devil

(Entry 1 of 2)

1 often capitalized : the personal supreme spirit of evil often represented in Christian belief as the tempter of humankind, the leader of all apostate angels, and the ruler of hell —usually used with the —often used as an interjection, an intensive, or a generalized term of abusewhat the devil is this? The devil you say!

2 : an evil spirit : <u>demon</u>

3a : an extremely wicked person : <u>fiend</u>

b archaic : a great evil

4 : *a person of notable energy, recklessness, and dashing spirit also : one who is mischievous* those kids are little devils today

5 : *fellow* —used in the phrases *poor devil, lucky devil*

6a : *something very trying or provoking* having a devil of a time with this problem

b : *severe criticism or rebuke : hell* —used with the I'll probably catch the devil for this

c : *the difficult, deceptive, or problematic part of something* the devil is in the details

7 : dust devil

8 *Christian Science* : *the opposite of Truth : a belief in sin, sickness, and death : evil, error*

between the devil and the deep blue sea

: *faced with two equally objectionable alternatives*

devil to pay

: *severe consequences* —used with the *there'll be the devil to pay if we're late.*" [9]

9 https://www.merriam-webster.com/dictionary/devil#synonyms Accessed 7th May 2020 @ 23:13

From 1787, the word 'devil' was **ALSO** used in a transitory sense, as you can see:

"devil

<u>verb</u>

*deviled or devilled; deviling or devilling\ 'de-və-liŋ , 'dev-liŋ *

Definition of devil (Entry 2 of 2)

transitive verb

1 : to season highly deviled eggs

2 : tease, annoy. [10]

WE can now surmise from (**BOTH**) the **ETYMOLOGY** and the **DEFINITION** that Devil/devil in a **ROOT SENSE** means "the personal supreme spirit of evil."

It is similar to the words archfiend, Beelzebub, fiend, Lucifer, Old Nick, Satan, Santa, and serpent.

QUESTION: So, what is **THE DEVIL?**

ANSWER: THE PERSONAL SUPREME SPIRIT OF EVIL.

---

10 https://www.merriam-webster.com/dictionary/devil#synonyms
Accessed 7th May 2020 @ 23:20

Do you have any further **QUESTIONS**?

Just to wrap things up. It is clear to see that **THE DEVIL** and **GOD** are titles, **NOT NAMES**, which means "**BOSS** or **CHIEF WITH SUPERNATURAL POWERS**" over some person or persons, some place or places, or some thing or things.

It is this that most of us need to realize.

ISN'T THE SUN OVER US ALL?

THE MOST HIGH OF ALL THE THINGS IN OUR DAILY VISION?

NATURE is often referred to as **GOD**, not "named God".

Which does make sense as **WE** should **ALL** be **AT ONE WITH NATURE** just as **WE ARE AT ONE WITH THE MOST HIGH**.

In **OUR ORIGINAL LANGUAGE WE SAY:**

NETER SHIL NETERU, OR NATURU SHIL NATURAAT, which means the **GOD OF ALL GODS (THE NATURE OF NATURE)**.

I didn't realize that I was writing about this subject today, but it has been a pleasure.

I have been so confused and so busy with **LIFE** lately, but I can never complain.

I have **CREATED** a **MONSTER BUSINESS** which is **GROWING QUICKER** than I could ever dream – I just need to find a way to try and catch up, but it is all good.

I just have one more **QUESTION** or one more line of questioning before I go.

I have often wondered.

WHY is a **DICTIONARY** called a **DICTION-ARY?**

Can anybody tell me?

When it has nothing to do with **DICTION**. Doesn't diction refer to speech as in dictation?

Shouldn't it have been called a **DEFINITIONARY**?

We do not **LOOK** up **DICTIONS**, do **WE**?

It's the **DEFINITIONS WE LOOK** for!

Isn't it?

This English **TONGUE** makes no **SENSE** if you ask me.

But who am I to **SPEAK**?

WHO are **WE**?

Let us move on to the next chapter. More will be **REVEALED**.

I would like to hand you over to Shawn Pereira, who will take you on a journey.

PEACE AND LOVE!

Kwadw(o) Naya: Baa Ankh Em Re A'lyun Eil

If you would like to find out more about Kwadw(o) Naya: Baa Ankh Em Re A'lyun Eil and his services, head to:

https://kwadwonayabaaankhemrealyuneil.gold/

ADVANCEMENT

GOD & THE DEVIL

None of your hip-hop artists are worshipping the Devil because the Devil does not exist unless it's self-created inside each individual.

This means each human has a polarity consciousness that allows a **GOD** and **DEVIL** to reside **WITHIN.**

And no God exists unless it's self-created inside each individual.

Most humans get their definition of a Devil from their parents and society at large and how much of the consensus reality they have bought into.

And it's usually from the Bible or Quranic perspective. Most people in America know about a Devil from a religious point of view, and most of your hip hop artists are themselves Christian or grew from a Christian or Muslim foundation.

The Devil was first introduced in your Garden of Eden Story in Genesis and he entered the garden and told Adam and Eve the truth that they would not die if they betook of the fruit. God did lie and told them that they would surely die. Look it up. So we are to assume the Devil is so evil, yet God lied, and your Devil told the truth, informing them like I am doing **NOW.**

Before that story was rewritten, it was Tehuti telling them the truth. And yes, your Devil was **TEHUTI.** Tehuti interfered like I am doing **NOW** and told the truth. Thus, I became the **DEVIL.**

Tehuti did promise to keep incarnating over and over again Having no mother and father until all of us are raised in frequency.

Don't be perplexed. It's not that convoluted. If I speak of Tehuti in the first person singular I decided by my own doing to be Tehuti today. And whenever I feel like it because he is of my family and lives within me.

Any of you can do this, but it comes with a certain responsibility. If you can't walk in the **SHOE**, you would not even attempt to try it on.

Advancement 3: God & The Devil

Listen carefully as I step off my **UNICORN** to hold your hand and walk you all through this as a Mr. Nobody.

Your Devil story is totally fabricated, and then we in the spirit realm actually had to create one to match what you humans were doing. You children of earth are very creative like your elders in the stars.

Listen closely. There is no Devil. It's just terminology created for polarity consciousness. No **GOD** exists.

God and the devil are levels of consciousness or energy force within each Enoshite.

When any of you uses its knowledge, power, and resources to help all humanity and love. It is using its God mind or power.

When any of you seek to be selfish and accumulate wealth and are boastfully displaying it as if the people did not give it to you, then you are using your devil mind. So paradoxically, your hip-hop artists and anyone that are behaving in this manner can be considered devil worshippers But so are the people buying the records and supporting these people. They, too, are devil worshippers.

Am I making this clear? Transparent as in "transmission from your parents," the **ELDERS?**

Devil worshipping is not what your religious people ascribed to it.

Those people within the secret society with their rituals are no different than Christians, Muslims, and Jews with their rituals. All of you have the power within you to activate your devil mind or your god mind. It is within each and every one of you.

All ritual signs and symbols are just permission slips. You all have the same power. If you give yours away, don't worry. That, too, is an illusion. You cannot truly lose your soul or give your power away.

All of you are **THE MOST HIGH GOD** and the most low devil, all at the same time. Don't hate those hip-hop artists because they are playing their game and know that they are their own god and their own devil.

Let me even the playing field by removing the devil as a person outside of all of you.

Now that all of us are devils, it has no more power over you. I have taken the **DEVIL** and **REDUCED** it to nothing.

Only a **TEHUTI** can do that. And with **LOVE**, I carry on. Now that all of us are **GOD**, it has no power over you also.

Listen again. Nobody can lose their soul. Listen, I said it. Nobody can lose their soul. There is only one thing in existence, only one moment in existence.

And all of us are one... you cannot lose to yourself.

You are everything, and everything is you. You cannot **LOOSE** your soul. You are **THE SOURCE**. You are **THE MOST HIGH** if you so desire. And the most low devil if you choose to be.

I will help to make all of you shine bright like the Sun **RE AMUN RAYAY**. Love, respect, and nurture one another.

For you are all **ONE**. The ReTurn Council.

GOD and THE DEVIL!

PEACE AND LOVE!

Shawn Pereira

You can find out more about Shawn and how he can help and assist by visiting his website:

https://www.returncouncil.com

ADVANCEMENT

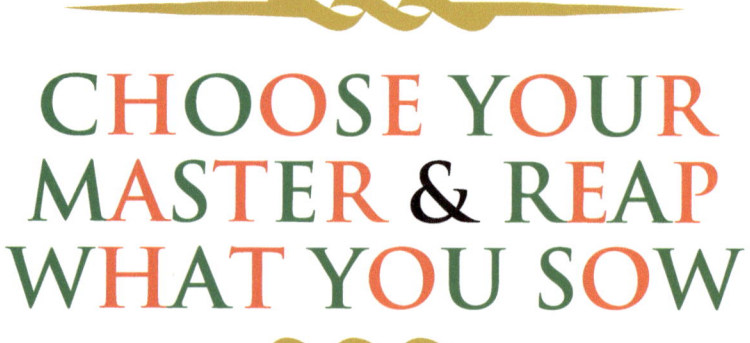

CHOOSE YOUR MASTER & REAP WHAT YOU SOW

Advancement 4: Choose Your Master & Reap What You Sow

Please allow me to introduce myself. My name is Daniel Owen Raine, I am a 24-year-old man from England, and I have been in the trenches with demons since I was young, battling the lies of the world with no weapons to battle with. Constantly losing has taught me a lot. I lost my mother at age 6, I have lost lots of money many times, and I have also lost fights in boxing which has humbled me and shown me many lessons. Most would've quit and given up on life by this point, but God gave me the strength to handle these situations and granted me wisdom as a result of the trials and suffering. It wasn't until later, when I found my authority in God, that things clicked, and those losses turned into the wisdom of righteousness, which subsequently turned into wins.

Throughout my life, I have always questioned reality, even during school when there was nothing but authority and pre-answered questions to regurgitate. The system we live in is based on false authority - fraud in the largest sense. It elevates the authority of man over his creator, and as a result, we have the corrupted system that we do. The lies of school are usually the start of the questioning for most, maybe even before, with the lies told, such as Santa and the Easter bunny.

Do you remember the first lie you were told?

How did you feel about it?

Was something instinctually wrong, but you didn't have the words to explain it?

I have felt all of these things and hope to give you some words of encouragement along your journey of truth-seeking. We are born into a world and groomed by lies from day one, so it is our imperative to destroy these strongholds and rebuild our minds in the knowledge of the truth of God so that our foundation is one built on a rock, not one built on sand. A solid foundation of righteousness vs. an unstable foundation of sin. Some get stuck in the pits of hell as a result of denying reality, and others climb back up to the surface on their journey to find the truth and, along their journey, pick up the knowledge and wisdom to help future generations escape the matrix of lies. Luckily God set me free from a young age, and now it's my duty to tell my fellow men and women the good news. Let's turn off the mainstream news for a moment and tune into the spiritual reality of God Almighty.

How many times have you found yourself acting without intention?

How many times have you felt yourself floating aimlessly, waiting for the opportunity to come?

Waiting for that **PERFECT** opportunity... it doesn't exist.

Opportunities are abundant and plentiful. Opportunities can lead to failure, but ensure you don't fail to act due to the fear of failure. **ACTION** alone **CREATES** an **OPPORTUNITY** for **EXPERIENCE**. This **EXPERIENCE** gives **WISDOM**. Failure is absolute proof of what not to do and therefore carves a narrower path for potential success. Success is absolute proof of what to do. (-8) and (+8) are both absolutely eight away from zero. Hence we gain wisdom during success and failure. Fail until you succeed. Have faith in God and know that if it isn't a success, then it's **NOT MESS.** Take the best and leave the rest. Failure means that you are not ready for your blessings, but it is there to show you how to be ready. You are now one step closer.

How many times have you put off a simple task to indulge in comfort for that split second longer only to allow the opportunity for action to slip away? Once you have triumphed over the demon of sloth and taken action, progress will occur. Focus, on top of intentional action, leads to greater progress. Less focused action is inefficient but still better than being idle.

If you have the urge to sing: **SING**.

If you have the urge to write: **WRITE**.

If you have the urge to move. **MOVE**.

And **KEEP IT MOVING.**

Act upon this moment of inspiration, and you will find passive income in relation to the skills of one's character. Over time you will grow into who you truly are as you express yourself through heavenly inspiration. The fruits of the spirit are available to us all so long as we follow the narrow path and act upon that God-given inspiration in the moment without judgment.

We are destined to slavery, however, we get to choose our master. Who do you choose to serve? **GOD** or **THE DEVIL**? God is unique expression in free will to bring **LOVE** on **EARTH**. The Devil is the mimicry and subversion of what is **GOOD** and

TRUE. This is the destruction of what is good and the subversion of what is to be on Earth. I choose to serve God Almighty, and as a result, I get freedom from the bindings of evil spirits and the actions that they cause. To work for something you hate is to be a slave. So then, why do the majority of us give eight hours a day to "just do our job" void of all passion and love? Mimicking the protocols of the dead entity known as a corporation. **MONEY** is the answer. Money is the master that enslaves the majority of man. Man cannot serve two masters, so mammon is the goal and highest force for them on Earth. God says, "My people are destroyed for lack of knowledge." They lack the knowledge of God and the freedom he provides when we serve him.

So then, why do the majority sell themselves for money? They are in slavery to their fleshly desires and believe in the lie that "there's limited energy," so, therefore, they must settle somewhere they hate "just to pay the bills." We live in a world of abundance. However, we reap what we sow. Therefore, we must sow action in line with our true purpose for the abundance to truly take place. Allowing God to guide your path allows for your truest expression at the cost of your sin. You and I and **EVERYONE ELSE** are created for different reasons. No corporation can define God's purpose for you.

We are destined to be a slave on this Earth, and as mentioned before, you choose your master. If you choose mammon, then you must note that if you are to choose this lifestyle and work purely for material gain, you will surely be a slave in sin, not a slave in righteousness. A slave in sin hates his daily tasks but loves his sin, so he cannot give up those daily tasks. A slave in righteousness **LOVES** their daily activities under God's holy command. One is not subject to a taskmaster under the command of God. It's an abundance of opportunity overflowing with the fruits of the spirits, such as **LOVE** and **JOY**. I already know the master that I choose.

DO NOT BE a slave to money whereby you sell your soul day in and day out, never building up skills outside the parameters of the corporate world. Everyone's inherent goal in life is happiness, but they fail to admit that only God can truly bring us happiness, and they convolute fleeting pleasures with **TRUE** happiness. If you trust in **GOD'S PLAN** and have faith, you will align your path with the will of **THE MOST HIGH**, which manifests the most congruent expression of your character created by **GOD**, **NOT** the subverted reality of the Devil that would exist if you sold your soul.

The paradox of life is that the more things you do, the more things you want to do. Whereas the common notion is that "doing things makes you tired" and is therefore used as an excuse to **NEVER**

EVEN TRY. This lie is propagated through the corporate world as many destroy their bodies in pursuit of money whilst subjugated to more lies that "once the body is broken, it cannot be repaired." This creates hopeless **SLAVES**. Your body was created perfectly. The environment we live in, however, is not currently perfect due to the influence of modern-day comfort and the race for profit over sustenance. This pattern permeates into the physical body as people use their bodies in a rush for profit whilst never caring to innerstand the structure or creation they reside within on this Earth. If you know yourself and the structure that you reside within, then you use your muscles in line with the said structure to create sustainable movement patterns that regenerate rather than deteriorate. A conscious focus on what is **GOOD** and **TRUE** leads us to an abundance in all dimensions of life and allows for growth under <u>**THE MOST HIGH**</u> to our greatest fulfillment.

PEACE AND LOVE!

Daniel Owen Raine

If you would like to find out more about Daniel Owen Raine and his services, head to:

https://danielowenraine.gold

ADVANCEMENT

TRIALS & TRIB-ULATIONS

Advancement 5: Trials & Tribulations

My name is Cyrlene. This is my introduction as a writer, just touching on some of the life experiences I've been through with the view to elaborate on these issues in my forthcoming series of books. I have been encouraged for years to write a book, and this is something I said I wanted to do one day, and now I am ready.

I grew up with a story that when I was one, I used to come downstairs to my mom and say, "man hurt hand" mom said I had red ring marks on my wrists, but no one was upstairs. I grew up with rastas telling me that they ran the ghost from the

Advancement 5: Trials & Tribulations

yard. Apparently, rastas went to the yard and chanted and used incense to cleanse the house.

I was bought up in the Midlands with a single-parent mother and one brother. My mom had us young, and she did her very best. We may not have had all the latest items that other children had, but we had a nice home, clean clothes, and we ate well. We would go to our grandparents Sis James and Grandad's house most weekends, which I thought of as the fun house, full of laughter, fun, and games. Going to church and Sunday school was part of that. My grandparents had a five-bedroom house, initially having 11 children, with some of those children having up to at least two dozen children. Having at least 25 people dinner on a Sunday wasn't unusual. You just hoped it wasn't your turn to be involved in the washing up. That house was full of my most-happiest memories. My grandparents passed away in 2016 and 2020, but it still feels quite raw. The house has been sold now, which is quite sad. It would have been nice to have kept it for a family home.

At the age of 7 me, my mom and brother moved into a new area called Northfields, and on the move-in day, whilst being sent to the chip shop, I was approached by six girls. The smallest one walked up to me and, out of nowhere, said, "I want you, don't I?" I replied that I didn't know her and that we had just moved into the area that day. Little skinny me, with my hair plaited with colored beads on the ends, was confused why this girl thought she knew me. She was there chatting away, trying to find an argument but wasn't really saying anything. After a while, I remembered the chips. Everyone was at the house unpacking and hungry. At this point, I knew what was more important, as a hungry man is an angry man, and I didn't want my mom to come looking for me. I told the girls I was going chippy for my mom. I crossed over the main road, went into the chip shop, and placed my order. I looked back across the road out of the window and saw the group of girls chatting, and I could see she was getting worked up as if they were egging her on. I wasn't confident because there were six of them. This day, I grew up very quickly and realized that this was to be the first of many fights. I knew when walking back that she was probably going to attack me, so I just told myself I might have to take a beating. I knew I couldn't back down because I would more likely be bullied whenever I saw any of them, which was very likely. I crossed over the main road, and as soon as she walked up to me and opened her mouth, I shoved the chips in her friend's chest and gave the girl a good beating, took back the chips, and scuttled back home, praying that they weren't going to decide to run me down before I reached my house.

I soon learned that the area was quite racist. I would get called all kinds of names just walking along the road. One day on my street, there was a family lying in their garden sunbathing on towels and loungers. As I walked by, I heard, "Black bastard." I replied, "Don't be hating on my skin, my tans all year round." I thought, what a cheek, you're there trying to get brown and calling me because I am as I am. As my mom says, I always have an answer for everything.

I obviously got the same at school but I was a good girl and held back a bit at first because mom didn't send me to school to fight. I can remember on a couple of occasions, I allowed people to hit me, and I didn't retaliate because I didn't want to get into trouble with mom. I can remember telling my nan Sis James a very stern Christian woman, what was happening at school and in my area, the name calling, kicking, and pushing I was being victim too. My nan said if they call you names, ignore them, but "If anyone lick yuh, lick dem back" that was all the green light and ammunition I needed.

On the road opposite my junior school, there was a grass patch with a small wall around it. This is where the school children would head after school as that's where the fights were held. I found myself on that green patch several times a week because people thought I was an easy target. I stood out because I was only one of a handful of dark people in the school. Eventually, after winning many fights, the name-calling and racism whittled out, and then the talk was that I was "alright for a black girl." I didn't enjoy fighting, but at the same time, I wouldn't back down or show any sign of weakness. People often mistake my size for weakness. I can remember I went to a house party in the area. I was walking back into the house after getting some air, and a man was walking out, and he said, "You black nigger" I don't remember thinking about hitting him; I just remember he was out cold on the floor. I was left astonished, looking at my right hand, figuring out how I managed to do that. From that day, no one really messed about with me in the area, although there was a time I was chased by a pack of dogs when riding my bike, and another time a swarm of bees chased me down the street. I ran into the house to my mom and said mom "even the bees are racist."

I was a very sporty child and won a lot of awards for running, dance, gymnastics, pool, and I was quite a good netball player. I was scouted at 11 for the over 16's county players. I also joined a modeling agency, so some weekends required me to be at home and not at my nan's. I could have been anything I wanted and was a carefree child, that was until my mom got a boyfriend.

Advancement 5: Trials & Tribulations

This man was really nice at first. He had a food shop, and I can remember his dumplings were the biggest I'd ever seen. He later gave up the food shop and focused on being an electrician, as this is a trade he was also in. As soon as he got his feet under the table, I soon learned that this man was not nice. I started to feel uncomfortable in his presence. He started to look at me in a particular way, sometimes trying to give me the eye.

My brother and I always spent time in my mom's bedroom, watching TV till we fell asleep, and then we would go to our own rooms. I can remember one day I was home on the weekend, and my brother was at nan's, and mom was working in the pub. I was at home alone with this man I looked up to as a father figure, someone that I could trust. He suffered with his sinuses and was not too well. We were in my mom's room, he was under the covers of the king-size bed, and I was on top in my nighty and dressing gown, watching TV with my feet pointing toward his head. All of a sudden, this man started to touch me, gently rubbing my leg up and down, slowly going higher and higher toward my knickers. I froze. I didn't know what to do in this situation. Although I didn't like it, I couldn't scream or shout at first. As he got closer to my crotch, I stiffened more and shut my eyes tight, and said in my head, God, please make him stop. As soon as I said that, the phone rang.

It was my mom checking up to see if everything was okay. At that point, I got up, ran into my room, and locked the door. The door was a little damaged. It had an old-fashioned thumb lock, it would lock, but if you pushed it as the wood was split, it could still open. This man forced the door to my bedroom and jumped on me. I was on the bed. I started fighting him and telling him to get off me. At one point, I said, "Get off me, else I'm gonna…" He interrupted, screaming in my face, "Tell her what, tell your mom what? He said, "girls like you end up as prostitutes…" I was 11 years old and a virgin. I didn't even know what a prostitute was.

After the first time at any opportunity, usually when I was downstairs in the early morning watching cartoons. He would come into the living room with his dressing gown naked and aroused underneath. He would try to rub himself up on me, and I would fight him in silence so that my mom wouldn't hear who was upstairs in bed.

I started to rebel because of what was happening in the home. I wanted to tell, but I was scared that I would not be believed. Anytime I knew I was to be left alone with this man, I would "run away." I didn't see it as that as far as I was concerned. I was at my dad's house. It's just that he wasn't aware of it as he had many a place he would lay his head. People would have my name on the road, saying that I was a bad child because I was running away and no one could find me when all I was doing was trying to keep myself safe from the predator in my home. It got to the stage where I stopped speaking to him. I think it was the time when he took this big belt buckle to my brother's head. I jumped on him and told him he wasn't our dad to be putting his hand on any of us. I realized that when I did not speak to him, he wouldn't try to trouble me in a sexual way. So I didn't and wouldn't say a word to him. I was always in trouble because mom said I had no manners because I wouldn't speak to the man. He wouldn't even get good morning from me. Why should a dirty paedo get any respect? My mom told me if I didn't speak to him, all the gymnastics, netball, etc., would stop, so they did.

Can you imagine not feeling safe in your own home as a little child? One day at the age of 12, I went home really late, there was a misunderstanding when mom thought I skipped school, but the teachers were on strike, I went home with the letter, but mom wasn't home. Knowing I should have stayed in the house, I went into town to the arcade which was on the ground floor of the snooker hall. I didn't know that my mom had spotted me. The next minute I look. My mom's coming towards the arcade with two constables. I hid and jumped behind a driving machine till they had finished searching all the floors of the building. I had never felt so embarrassed in my life. Everyone was laughing at me because my own mom called the police on me. I said I wasn't going back home that night, but when it got about 11 pm, I knew mom would be worried and decided to go back. I went home but was scared to knock on the door because the dutty man's van was outside. I peeped through the window, and I could see my mom sitting there with the phone looking through the newspaper. Eventually, at 4 am, I went into the house with the help of a neighbor who was coming in from his night shift. We had a chat. I showed mom the letter from the school. She told me not to get up for school because I wouldn't have had enough rest. I thought mom was going to give me a beating, but she was more relieved that I was home safely. At around 7 am, the dirty man starts to shout in the house, comes into my room, and tells me to get up and go to school. Ranting throughout the house, he went to the outside toilet where he kept some of his electrical goods, he got three threads of wire from the roles he had, cut them, and started to whip me all over my body whilst he was doing this he was ripping off my knickers and trying to insert his fingers into me. After the beating, I went to school sobbing my eyes out. I couldn't stop crying; my body felt like it was on fire. I had red raised whip marks all over my body. My dance teacher saw me, and that was it straight social services, and I was never to return home again.

I was placed in a children's home. The first day I went in, the whole place stunk of glue. The children in the home did everything to get high, Tipp-Ex, pens, anything. This was the first time I saw this kind of thing. The first night I shared a room with a girl. She had an aerosol of some kind and sniffed that with a towel, next minute, I saw her looking all weird, and her lips went blue. I was scared as hell, panicking, not sure what I should do… I remember her waking up in the morning without getting out of her bed, putting on makeup with her two black feet sticking out from under the sheets. I soon came to realize how other people lived, a different side of life that was alien to me.

I didn't like it when I was in care. I didn't want to be seen with the children or do any activities with them, I felt embarrassed, and so I always opted for the money instead of horse riding or any activity they had planned.

At one point, they were trying their best to foster me with a family. They placed me with a Caucasian family who had young children that made racist comments on the first day I arrived. Not a good start, and I instantly looked at the parents for their children's behavior. They didn't care about me; I was nothing but another income stream outside of their market stall business.

I didn't want to be there. I didn't feel comfortable, the cultural differences were so apparent, and I was in a different area so far away from anyone or anything I knew. I would wake up, leave the house and return when it was time to go to sleep. This social worker seemed hell-bent on fostering me out and was not listening to what I wanted. They then tried to foster me with a woman who looked strict as hell. At that point, I went on the run from the care system, doing what I wanted, still seeing family, going skating, and sitting on carnival floats. I didn't want to fit into another family. If it was not my family, I wasn't interested. By this time, I had already learned that I could get my own place without the fostering, so this was my plan. I moved in with a couple of girls, Susan and Annmarie, lovely girls that I had known for a while. I started shoplifting to pay my way. I would steal an item of clothing for £300 and sell it for half price. I would use it for rent, food, and what I would need to live. That money would go far, and when it ran out, I would do the same again. I never stole before, but this was a way for me to get by and pay my way. After a while, I eventually returned to the children's home and used to get praised when I returned from doing as I pleased at the weekends.

Advancement 5: Trials & Tribulations

At 14 years old, I moved into a hostel, and instead of going to school, I got a job in a bar-tacking factory in the area, putting bows, etc., on garments and underwear. I started buying little bits and bobs with my wages for the flat I would be getting. I felt so behind with my studies at school, leaving home, etc., I didn't think there was any point going.

At this age, I started going to blues parties to listen to music. I generally got looked after because the people there knew my mom and dad, so people were quite protective of me. I remember catching the 12:01 am train to Nottingham to go to Blue Lagoon Blues and catching the 6:30 am train back to Leicester, going in to have a quick wash, changing my clothes, and getting to work for 8 am. I got my first 1-bed flat at 15 years old, a ground-floor flat in a large Victorian house. I was really pleased with the size of it and the fact it had a garden was amazing.

The feeling of being away from your family at such a young age, trying to navigate through life, wasn't easy. There are many influences that come into your life, good and bad. I preferred to be around elders as people my age couldn't teach me anything. I was thirsty for knowledge and learning about life. I already had ethical principles and morals instilled in me from my mom and the fear of God from the Christian side of the family. I knew right from wrong and have always been concerned about how the creator will view my ways and behaviors. I have always tried to live good with people and treat people how I would like to be treated, but I soon found out that not everyone is the same.

Some of the worst experiences of my life were in that flat. I started to learn about people and their dirty ways. So-called friends, you let into your home for them to steal from you, envious of the little bit I had. People always seemed to be chatting my name. I couldn't understand it until one false rumor got me really upset, sobbing. I had a dog called Lex at the time, and she could be very affectionate and has been known to cry with me, but on this occasion, she was rough with me hitting me with her nose as to say, "Stop the raasclaat crying." That's the message I got anyway. I soon stopped, and a thought came into my mind that has never ever left me to this day.

If people are taking the time to make up lies about me, that means I must be significant in their lives, so, therefore, it makes me special, so it didn't feel so bad looking at it in that way.

In this property, I attempted to take my life on three occasions, the last attempt, I was astounded when I woke up at my friend's house in the country with his family around me. I was there for four days out cold. When I woke, I wanted to cry because I was still here. I shouldn't have woken up with the cocktail of alcohol and tablets I had taken. I wanted out. The fact that I woke up made me realize that I am here for a **purpose.** I think I had come across the verse in the bible that you don't get any forgiveness for taking your own life. I cried and apologized to **The Most High** for what I did and promised I wouldn't do it again.

At the age of 28, I received a nine-year prison sentence, released in Dec 2003

I got mixed up with the wrong person after being wrongfully evicted from my home. I was vulnerable and felt like I had nowhere to turn, and I ended up serving four and a half years of a nine-year sentence, starting at Holloway Prison and moving around to several prisons around the country. During this time, I focused on education; I didn't do very well at school and wanted to get some qualifications under my belt so I had a good chance of getting a job when I was released. I exhausted the education system coming out with 42 NVQs from hair, nails, computers, sports, bookkeeping, and the lot. I was in the gym every day. I loved it in the gym, becoming a gym orderly and minibus driver for the last year or so of my sentence.

I was involved in some peer research in regard to what prevented female prisoners from accessing education, training, and employment once being released into the community from prison. I would hold focus groups and record the sessions with a facilitator that came into the prison. I was paid £5 per hour for my work which came in handy when I was released.

I was released on the 18th Dec 2003. I relocated to London, first to a hostel in the Brick Lane area. I was glad to be in London but felt a little lost in the big city. I had saved up a few hundred pounds, but that went very quickly as I had to buy some clothes, a decent jacket, and bits to be comfortable in my little room. Coming out so close to Christmas meant there was not much support for me; everywhere was closed, and I had no money from the benefits people. I had applied for a job on the 10th Dec whilst I was still inside and learned I had been short-listed for an interview on the 16th Jan. For me, it was vital I got this job for a number of reasons, getting to know others, to find my way around London and to keep things moving as I could feel the depression setting in being in that room. I went for the interview, and as soon as I got back to the hostel, they called me and told me I was successful. I cried my eyes out, the relief!

The job was in HM Prison Send in Woking, working on the resettlement unit supporting women that were about to be re-leased into the community. Two positions later, within four years, I worked my way up to team leader, earning over £32,000 per year, which I am extremely proud of. This was a good time for me. I felt like I was becoming my own person and didn't feel like such a failure in life. I totally turned my life around, living in London and on a good wage.

Unfortunately, in 2009 I was in a car accident on the motorway, which changed my life forever. Coming to a near-death experience, you re-evaluate your life, you retrace your last steps, who you saw, who you didn't see, and what you should have said. I was not coping very well; my depression had grown deeper, and my health started to deteriorate. In addition, I had some issues in the workplace with my manager, who was not happy when I applied for a management role. Workplace bullying put me into further depression, having to deal with the union and file reports. The succession of issues was taking a toll. I wasn't eating, I wasn't sleeping, and flashbacks from the accident were in my dreams and when I was wide awake. I had a weird taste in my mouth for months and got very tearful and angry quickly.

They didn't give me the management job that I applied for, but the person that did get the job couldn't do the job and my manager thought it was okay to bring the work to me to do, but I refused. My manager at the time was doing all kinds of underhanded things. It was quite unbelievable. In one of my appraisals, I told her to her face and gave her numerous examples of how she was trying to bully me. She seemed shocked that I was so brazen and direct, knowing she had to write it down. She had to take a couple of breaks. I think she felt intimidated, which was my intention if I'm honest. I felt like giving her a taste of her own medicine. I was basically waiting for them to sack me, but they didn't have any reason to, as I did my work, and I did my job extremely well, according to all my previous appraisals and reports. They were outstanding up to the point when I applied for a management role. I was made redundant from my job in 2010, not long after they got rid of my manager. The union was sick of the complaints about her behavior over the years. She was Jamaican/Bajan like me, nice at first but switched when I dared to apply for a job outside of her team.

I began to isolate myself and cut everyone off. I felt like I was losing it and did not want to be around people. My friends would call me with their problems. I was that person to give advice and problem-solve. I felt hurt because I was in such a bad place, and no one even recognized that anything was wrong with me. I stopped going out, socializing, and picking up calls. I didn't understand why I was feeling the way I was; I felt scared.

Beginning to wonder what life was about, I wanted to know my purpose and wondered if there really was a God. I spent my time looking into these things. I began to look at my life, how I spent my last year, last hours, and minutes before the accident. I knew I was not myself and felt frightened and untrusting of people. I felt the less time I spent around people, the less information I had to digest, the less noise in my head. I spent time at my mother's house, basically in my room, and not leaving the house to visit friends or family. I just felt down. I could see my mom was worried because usually, I would be all over the place visiting friends and family.

In 2012 I was assessed by NHS, and I had another assessment at Harley Street. The results came back within two weeks of each other, and they both said I was suffering from severe post-traumatic stress disorder as a direct result of the accident. I had no idea an accident could make you feel such a way. I've already been through so much but always managed to get up and get on with things, but this was different. I had been previously diagnosed with manic depression in my teenage years also. I try not to take on their labels, and I don't take their medications either. As a teenager, I was ill, and they gave me some tablets, and when I read the slip inside about the side effects, I was startled and dashed the tablets in the bin and looked at alternatives, natural ones.

I have had several bouts of counseling, and I even paid £5,000 for eye movement desensitization and reprocessing and then went on to tapping. I just wanted to get out of that bad place I was in. The waiting lists on the NHS are an issue. You have to wait so long, and if you don't get the correct referral and type of therapy you need, it's a waste of time. This was my experience.

I was raped twice by the same man in my flat, once at 16, and he came back again when I was 17 years old. This had the most devastating effect on my life and affected me severely up until my 40th birthday. When I realized how long I had allowed this man to have this negative effect on me. I reported this rape for the third time on the 27th of August 2012 as I needed closure. He needs to be held accountable for what he did to me.

Not soon long after reporting this, I went through a very traumatic time where I was visited by a spirit, a spirit that was trying to trouble me in a sexual way in my sleep. I now know this to be called the incubus spirit. I know many people may be disbelieving what I'm saying right now, rightly so because I didn't want to believe this was the case either. This was until I had no choice but to believe it was really happening. I went through every emotion you could think of. I couldn't eat, I lost weight, and I was confused and scared. As you would never think this kind of thing would happen to you, you see it in films and on TV.

My traumas as a child were something I had not dealt with properly; I couldn't really speak about them. The first help or support that I had was in prison. This woman that I thought came to help me through my traumatic past, sat there like a dummy, barely acknowledging anything I said. I was in there 15 minutes and called the officer to come and put me back in my cell so I could go and talk to my wall because I would get more of a response.

Over the years, I had many counseling sessions, but the technique where they don't respond or talk to you did not work for me. I found them frustrating. I needed someone to help me get to the bottom of why I was still feeling the way I was after so many years. I need support mechanisms and tools to be able to identify ways of coping when I am triggered. Not a dummy thinking I can go at 3 pm on a Tuesday and talk on tap and then leave for another week to think about those problems that were bought back to the surface. I think it is only us that can heal ourselves.

In 2018 I became physically ill; I was diagnosed with complex post-traumatic stress disorder. I was going through so many different issues. My body was stressed, I had multiple ulcers, and I had a throat problem where my esophagus wouldn't function properly. I struggled to drink water. These symptoms I have had before.

I lost my grandparents, and this had a devastating effect on me in a number of ways. There is the obvious, but there were devastating blows to me and how I felt left out of the funeral arrangements being the "first grandchild," they missed me and went to the sibling down from me. You see, from a child, I noticed certain things like there was no father named on my birth certificate, but there was on my brother's, who was 18 months younger than me. I noticed I looked different; all my family on my "father's" side had a particular look.

I knew deep down that he wasn't my "father," and finally, at the age of 13, I decided to ask my mom. Her response was, "I don't want to speak about it" that response told me everything. I asked for a number of years and got nothing. I asked every member of my family on every side and got nothing. This affected my relationship with my mom. I felt betrayed. I felt everyone around was fake and just keeping up pretenses. More than anything, I just wanted to know where I came from. I wasn't looking for a dad. I never had any father figure in my life, so what you don't have, you don't miss. This scenario was the main reason I stopped watching TV because there were so many programs that would trigger me and get me into a state where I was longing to know who I was. One day I got down on my knees, cried, and prayed to the creator to lead the way so I could find out where I came from. I held that faith for a few decades and never had a doubt in my mind that I would find out. In Nov 2019, **The Most High** answered my prayers in the most amazing way, and I feel like this lifted a lot of weight from my shoulders.

This short overview of my life has many stories within it. The traumas of my childhood included child abuse, rape, suicide attempts, violence, domestic violence, and systematic racism. There are so many things I have not spoken about in this short extract that involve relationships, domestic violence, prison scenarios. I was a drug dealer for a while. I even went through a scenario that would make fatal attraction look like a fairy tale. A family broke into a house and tied me up to the cistern pipe in the outside toilet, waiting for my partner to come on his lunch from work. On another occasion, a crazy woman broke into the house with surgical gloves with a view to hang me from the banister.

For years I have had friends and family telling me I must write a book. I have been approached by reporters and magazines offering me a fee to tell particular stories that had ended up in court, I refused back then as it was my personal stuff, and If anyone was going to write about it, it was going to be me.

Now I'm ready to do so, life is so short, and I feel the urge to do this now.

I know some of these stories will upset a few people. Those that know me will be shocked at some of these revelations that I am to reveal. This is in no way to harm or embarrass anyone. I just need it out in the open. I want to help others that feel they have been dealt a bad hand in life.

I feel it is important to record our lives as a way to express ourselves. For me, this is healing but, at the same time, upsetting going back into my past in this way. It has bought up so many emotions.

Many things are kept in the closet, family secrets, dirty secrets where abuse and rape are involved. There is a stigma to keep quiet about it like the victims are at fault in some way and should feel ashamed. I have a big problem with this. It has been on my conscience for years because I know how rife child abuse within families is. I've seen videos come through my WhatsApp, and those images imprinted on my mind, the most disgusting things that two and five-year-olds are exposed to.

Having your innocence taken away like this is soul-destroying. Many of the victims become abusers themselves because they think it is normal. I've seen it, and I have also identified a child who was being abused in her home by her father by a few words she said to me. I mentioned my fears to the neighborhood, and within weeks this little girl was in trouble at school doing inappropriate things to boys her age in school. I was right. The father was troubling the child. I also learned that the child's mother was only 14 when she had this little girl.

I am tormented at what I am doing at the moment because I feel that the prevention of child abuse is something that I should be championing and putting my efforts into.

Until **we reach our goal, our purpose, our destination, until our job is done.**

Our time here is very precious – wouldn't you agree?

So where am I now?

Since the lockdowns, I have been looking into law and our human rights. As a teenager, I preferred to be around elders. I gained a lot of knowledge about the government and their future plans, back then it seemed a life-time away, but as time passed things would unfold into our reality.

What we are seeing now, with the lockdowns and plan-demic comes as no shock to me, however, I'm astounded at the number of people that can't see through it. All I can say is they have been hypnotized in some sort of way or oblivious to the realities of life.

Initially, I spent a lot of my time trying to let people know the truths and dangers of the plan-demic, as more information was being revealed.

I know I have saved a few people from taking the poison, and changed a few people's minds which I feel good about. It was such a great feeling when I got messages from people who expressed their gratitude for posts I shared as it opened their eyes, others apologized for not believing initially, then the penny dropped.

I remember a post on Facebook that involved nurses and those that worked in the **NHS**, who thought they had to take the shot to keep their jobs. Months later I went to Leicester and a gentleman hugged and thanked me for my post due to the fact I directed him to a telegram group with doctors and nurses in the same position where he could get the right support and advice.

I am now at the stage where I don't even want to talk about it or see it. My focus is on me and my future. I am not interested in what is happening out there, I mean, the mainstream media isn't telling you what is really happening, it's pure lies and fabrication being fed through that square manipulative box.

I just tap in now and then to see where they are at with their plans, in order for me to know what I should be doing at any particular time.

Right now my priority is to free myself from the system, setting up my own trust, taking care of my own estate, and getting myself out of all the contracts that I have been entered into without my consent.

What we focus on becomes our reality, so in these serious times, it's about getting ourselves right. We can manifest and bring into fruition what it is we want to see in our future.

We all have free will to do as we wish and have access to the internet and can research. If people do not care enough to look for the answers, then that is on them.

I am in a much more **positive** place?

It's amazing that through all the trauma of what's happening with the plan-demic, one can feel at peace and have no fear in what may or may not happen. Learning to trust the process and just to focus on the things that you want.

I am now ready to write and share my stories, hoping to inspire, encourage and give strength to those that may have or are still experiencing any of these issues or anything similar.

I have been through many trials and tribulations. Sometimes, I wonder what I have done to deserve the cards I have been dealt with. They say God doesn't give you more than you can handle, and I am a living testimony of that. I give thanks for the strength and tenacity instilled in me to overcome the many barriers and still remain sane (most of the time) and still have love in my heart for others.

This life, at times, can be a **nightmare**, and sometimes **one** can find themselves in a situation which they have no control over – often, it can lead to abuse, rape, violence, and racism, which can lead to negativities like depression, self-harm, and even suicide attempts.

What I have learned, which I strongly felt to share with you, is that life is a **test.** We are all going to go through something. It's how you deal with it and what you take from it that matters. Each day you wake up, take it as a new start, a new beginning. Remember to give thanks and gratitude for the many blessings we do have, for the simple things in life.

In **this life**, **we are all** confronted with **trials** and **tribulations** which can **make** or **break us** – you **see**, it is **our experiences** that define **us**, which give **us our wisdom**, which forms our very **being!**

I have learned to be comfortable in my own space, sit in silence, meditate and visualize the things I want. I am a very passionate person, so I put time and effort into the things I want to achieve. Once you put that time in, you will see doors opening; things will start to take shape. You just have to make that start.

Always trust the process, and don't allow anyone to steer your path or the direction you have decided to go, particularly if you feel things are not moving as quickly as you have hoped. Patience is key.

Please **know** that with **love** and **support**, anything is possible. **Self-love** should always be a prerequisite. If we do not have the capability to **love ourselves**, how could **we** ever **love** anybody else? **You see** my point?

We are **divine beings** made in <u>**The Most High's**</u> image, and I know we are put here to support one another physically and mentally. We are here to show compassion and love for one another. That is what our whole being is about.

What I have realized is that **we** should always remain **positive** even in times of trauma – **one** can always find **strength**. Sometimes **you** just need to find the **courage** to **face your fears** and **anxieties**.

I turned 50 in 2021, and I feel grateful and blessed that I have reached such an age. I know I have so much to give, and I believe these short stories resonate with many women. I think of life as a journey. Nothing is going to run smoothly. We are all going to have problems and issues until the next one arises. Set your daily routines so you start your day right, pray, meditate, sun gaze, say or write positive affirmations, and read or listen to a chapter a day. For me, these things are vital. I don't do all every day, maybe 2 or 3, but I truly believe they help. I also believe that I am protected by a higher force that has a greater plan for me, and in 2023, I'm about to explore that. Watch this space.

Where there is faith, there is hope!

Although I have talked about some of my traumatic past here, throughout it all, I have had many amazing successes. Yes, you can still achieve through your trauma. I will talk about how I managed to strive throughout my traumatic life in my **next Chapter: Getting things done.**

PEACE AND LOVE!

Cyrlene

Feel free to visit my website and see how I can help you to **EMPOWER YOUR – SELF**.

https://cyrlene.gold

ADVANCEMENT

6:

INTEGRITY

Advancement 6: Integrity

Photo by Brett Jordan[11]

According to the Oxford Dictionary, integrity is the quality of being honest and having strong moral principles.

"Firm adherence to a code of especially moral or artistic values: INCORRUPTIBILITY." - Merriam-Webster Dictionary.

Synonyms: Honesty, Honor, Probity.

---

11 https://www.pexels.com/photo/brown-wooden-blocks-with-number-10815211/

I'm Akinsola Olayinka, a freelance graphic designer from Nigeria. I run an Agency focused on publishing and branding for authors.

I believe in learning and continual improvement (**KAIZEN**), and I use the knowledge gained to help my clients get a better edge in their respective markets.

According to an adage in my local language, a tiger will always give birth to another tiger. I often ask myself, do I need to be monitored or paid to do the right thing? I realize that the value instilled in me by my parents from childhood goes a long way in determining how I go on about living my life. That's not to say that you won't need to reinvent yourself at a certain point in your life. I have often wondered if I would have ended up differently if my parents had not instilled these values in me.

However, you can't rule out the importance of self-discovery. Also, you can't rule out the place of contentment in the journey of integrity. There will be a time when you will need to choose what you want to believe in and how you want people to see you. There is no self-discovery without you finding your way to happiness, and you have to be happy with yourself right from within. You will be tried and tested; even if you fail, you still have to pick yourself up.

There can be no integrity without values and belief systems. You can have negative values, which automatically translates to you lacking integrity; you can also have positive values manifest as genuine integrity. Integrity transcends beyond being honest and not lying at all. It encompasses all areas, including being responsible in the way you spend. Integrity is being accountable, even for your mistakes, when it's most inconvenient. How do you determine what is right? Knowing that you're not infallible and guarding against it is where integrity starts.

As integrity is all-encompassing, you'll need to consider the following:

A. WHAT DO YOU DO WHEN NO ONE IS WATCHING?

In these modern times, the number one problem we have is hypocrisy. Many seek validation, either on social media or elsewhere, that they forget who they actually are or what they stand for. I often ask myself, "Would you do things differently when there is no oversight or monitoring?" Of course, I would. Let's not be too sure, though. Let's look at this from a holistic point of view later in this chapter, and we are using real-life situations.

B. HOW MUCH DOES INTEGRITY COST?

"What money cannot do, more money will do it!" - A popular Nigerian politician

You cannot compromise true integrity. Therefore, you cannot, under any circumstances, compromise your integrity. I often think ahead - I have a friend who would often say I like overthinking. However, you can't lose your guard when your integrity is on the line. Money buys everything, but it shouldn't be your integrity. If you have never been tempted with a lot of money - I repeat, a lot of money, to do what ought not to be, then you should prepare mentally ahead for it. I'm not kidding. That day will come, and you can't predict what you will do when you're staring at that stark reality if you have never prepared for it.

Let me tell you a story. Let me tell you about someone I would call Mr. A living in country X. It happens that Mr. A was assigned to a supervisory role in a state election in country X. Now, country X is a corrupt country where only money matters. The situation is tense for Mr. A as he can't even provide adequately for his family. As an official, Mr. A was tempted with a huge sum of cash to influence the result of the election. Even when Mr. A knows that if he accepts the money, there will be "no consequences" at the end of the day, yet Mr. A still cunningly declines. You can't decline brazenly, as you can end up being a target since you did not do their bidding. Hence, Mr. A was shrewd about it. So, there will always be times when your integrity will be tested.

As they would say in my culture, "Remember the son of who you are."

C. HOW LONG DOES INTEGRITY PERSEVERE

How determined are you to be upright even when everything is not working out for you? Let's be honest. You can't always have it under control. Most will break under pressure (or extreme pressure). Hence if you are not determined to stick with your values no matter what, you can make a compromise when you feel like you can no longer take it. There will always be light at the end of the tunnel, but how determined are you to go through the tunnel - right to the very end of it?

D. INTEGRITY IN SERVICE DELIVERY

If you are a service provider, you always need to underpromise and over-deliver. This cannot be overemphasized enough.

As a service provider myself, what I always do is add a little something for my clients to the services that I provide without being asked. It's not quite easy, but it will help you in the long run. Even if you are not a service provider, it's in your place to maintain a high moral standard.

You also need to keep deadlines and appointments. Being in the creative industry, it's sometimes not predictable, and you may find yourself lacking in this aspect. As I have learned recently, you need to be realistic and be straight about it if you think you won't be able to meet up.

HOW TO LOSE YOUR INTEGRITY

1. STANDING AS SURETY

One of the riskiest things to do is stand as a guarantor or surety for another person. Not to say you shouldn't vouch for someone else; however, how well do you know the other person? If the other person were to fail to meet up with his/her obligation regarding the matter for which you are standing in the gap, do you know that your integrity will be questioned? Most especially in such cases where it is obvious that the person absconded or rejected outrightly to be accountable. It says so much about the kind of person that you trust or you associate with. And that is why in a criminal case, there is a difference in the interpretation of the meaning of a friend and an acquaintance. If you call someone your friend or you're vouching for another person's character, there can be no excuse or claim of ignorance if things go the other way. As someone I know will say, "You are the equivalent of the five people that you hang with."

2. CONDONING IRRESPONSIBLE SPENDING FROM YOUR PARTNER

As much as you can go to any length to please your partner, you shouldn't tolerate some level of irresponsibility regarding financial shrewdness or accountability. It can cause a lot of problems. One of the basics of economics is to differentiate between **WANTS** and **NEEDS**. If you have a partner that's not wise about spending, it's best if you address it head-on right from the start. If you fail to do that, sooner or later, you're going to have a very messed up financial statement. Just imagine how much pressure you will be putting on yourself if you have no savings (as a back-up for rainy days). You could end up taking credit when you don't need to. Once you start taking credit for the wrong reasons, it's just a matter of time before you lose it all.

Advancement 6: Integrity

3. FAILING TO MEET DEADLINES

As said before, always under-promise and over-deliver. Once you start missing deadlines, it won't take long before your promises are questioned. Anything you say after that point will not be believed. I'm talking from a place of experience. Although, we all try to improve ourselves after our first bitter experience. However, what I've found out is that it's always good to be upfront that you won't make it instead of trying to meet the deadline when you know it's not feasible.

4. NOT SETTING BOUNDARIES

The first thing you need to do in any relationship is to set boundaries. I'm not kidding. That doesn't mean you should go read the "10 commandments" to people. No! That's not what I mean. It means you should set boundaries within your mind such that you don't allow people to go past them. I'll explain. When you don't have a set of rules guiding you and what you want, you don't have a philosophy to follow. Have you ever wondered why most of the arguments in a relationship come from money issues? While one of the partners is a good money manager, the other may be a reckless spender. Budgeting is one of the easiest ways to set boundaries in this situation. Be sure to lay out the plan, and both agree to it. It will save you a lot of headaches and sleepless nights. If you don't do this, sooner or later, you may end up in debt.

Talk about courtesy and how your partner treats others. Boundaries must be set too. Whatever bad behavior your partner or someone very close to you exhibits in public will definitely rub off on you.

5. NOT DOING DUE DILIGENCE

You could be humiliated by the simplest things. You must examine everything carefully before passing it over or moving on. I'm sure we've all heard certain questions like, "Are you sure you checked this well?" By the time you are asked this question, the confidence/trust the person had in you before that instance has been reduced by nearly 50%. Most cases of fraud were successful because someone failed to check well. And great catastrophe has been avoided because someone paid attention.

By the way, what is diligence?

According to the Oxford dictionary, diligence is "careful and persistent work or effort." Please pay attention to the word **CAREFUL**. If we want to equate this attribute to some highly specialized fields like surgery or air traffic control, then you will appreciate this trait. The world's most successful surgeons are those who take that extra care in doing what they do. A popular saying is that "The devil is in the detail." If Ben Carson had been reckless, then he wouldn't be as successful in his field as he is today. Even when he was a student, he studied carefully and diligently.

I have read a story where a mid-air collision between two passenger airplanes was avoided by a split-second decision. Even one of the pilots said he saw the other plane so close as he glided past his aircraft. How did this happen? Just a change of shift where a more careful person took over the control of the radar prevented what would have been one of the worst accidents in the aviation industry in that decade. This single event changed a whole lot in the aviation industry, including how air traffic controllers were trained.

6. BE CAREFUL WHO YOUR ROLE MODEL IS

If you emulate people blindly, you can be led astray. You must have a mind of your own for you to discern between what is good and what is bad all the time. When you see someone you hold in high esteem being implicated in many questionable events, you need to re-evaluate why you hold this person in such a position. I've seen situations where a person who is

Advancement 6: Integrity

highly regarded by another falls short of several metrics. Not to say that there is a perfect woman out there; however, we all know that there are some things people do that really fall below the line. For example, I've been reading about a certain "rich guy" who has been sleeping with women, including the wife of his friends. What does that tell you about the person's character? You wouldn't be surprised if you see other skeletons if you dig deeper. In these modern times, when deceit reigns supreme, you cannot just follow anyone blindly, let alone always believe that whatever decision they make is always right, and that's what you want to emulate.

7. CAREER CHOICE

Have you ever seen a politician that doesn't lie? While I'm not saying there aren't good politicians, it will be difficult for most people to believe politicians due to several events that we've witnessed. Even during the Roman Empire, politicians were not that trusted. You can dig into the history. Needless to say, the modern day is when all sorts of shady things happen. Come to think of it, the scandals never end. And this has made a lot of people not believe in them. As soon as you go political, I'm sure most people will start to question what you stood for over the years. They are always seen as people with ulterior motives. While there are 'good' people in politics, how many people trust them?

Another example of such is like saying a director of a spy agency will always speak the truth. Please, what planet did you just drop from? There are some careers that you take up that you are expected to lie.

8. FEAR

If you are always fearful, then it's easy to compromise your standard under pressure. Statements like 'He made me do it' have never been admitted in a court of law as a good reason/excuse for messing with the law. One wrong decision under fear can jeopardize your whole career and character. Take, for example, couples who are not in bed with their partners crime but are too afraid to speak up. They often end up with 'lesser sentence,' don't they? However, they are never considered innocent when the bubble finally bursts. They are always regarded as an accomplice for not speaking up, likewise, in a corporate environment with predatory behavior. You must be fearless sometimes so that you don't succumb to pressure or fear. At the end of the day, and after succumbing, it may not even work well in your favor. "Que sera sera."

KEYS TO INTEGRITY

1. PITY/EMPATHY

A person who is cruel can never be a person of integrity. There is a trait I have noticed about those that scam others for a living; they are usually manipulative and not empathetic toward the other person. It is always about them. Without empathy, it is a whole lot easier to cheat people. Will you ever consider somebody who cheats or engages in various vices to be a man/woman of integrity?

2. PERSONAL RESOLVE/RESOLUTION/REINVENTION

No matter the values your parents teach you, there is a place for reinventing yourself. What do you want out of life? What do you want people to know you for? There will be some personal values that you imbibed from your parents. It is up to you to keep on defining who you are, what you want to stand for, and what you want people to know you for. It's not easy, I know. However, it is worth it in the long run. Whatever you do has a way of coming back to you, and that's exactly what your children will emulate too.

3. REALISTIC CONSCIOUSNESS

You must be conscious and intentional about everything you do. Why not ask yourself if the choices or decisions you're making will make your personality be questioned in the future? As I've said earlier, whatever you do has a way of coming back to you. You have to be conscious and intentional about what you do every day.

4. HUMILITY

You must be humble to take corrections and learn. Nobody is an island of knowledge. There will be times when you will be corrected about your actions. You should be humble enough to take it and make amends. Otherwise, you will meet a bigger fall in the future if you are arrogant.

HOW TO MAINTAIN YOUR INTEGRITY

1. CONTENTMENT IS BLISS

Your first line of defense against dishonesty is contentment. There is a difference between complacency and contentment. Don't mix it up! It's easier to make hard decisions when you are content with what you have. Lack of contentment is greed. And when you're greedy, there is nothing you wouldn't do to satisfy your unquenchable thirst for what you want. I remember when I was in college, there was this roommate of mine who would steal from you if you were careless. He didn't lack money. In fact, he had more upkeep money being sent to him than any of us. What was his problem? Greed! You heard that right. This guy was very greedy and always wanted all of the good things. Hence, no matter what he had, he was never satisfied and would go to any length to get what he wanted. It took a while before we figured out he was the thief; however, we had paid the price for trusting the wrong person. When his cover was finally blown, we never looked at him the same way. Even though he was part of our clique, we were never comfortable around him, and everyone avoided him. Nobody wants to have anything to do with a thief, you know.

When I was younger, my father would put us in charge of disbursing cash for his project. I'm talking about real money that is far more than what people think children of our age will have access to (I will always value this lesson). It made us immune to the negative attraction that comes with the need for "big money." Even though we didn't have everything we wanted, we were content, and never for once did we steal from him. That's good, right? Hold on, let's dive in. This happens a lot of time, and if you are from a family where your dad and mom are not together, it's easy for you to make friends. You don't want to be around the house all the time - stepmother issues; also, some of the new friends you make are not the good ones. Phew, it was a dilemma. I had some of my "friends" then that would suggest that I steal from my father. My response was always, "I don't do that." Do you know why? I was content with what I had. Even though I may lack a lot of things as of then; however, that won't make me do that kind of thing. I have been in charge of cash flow in several of my previous workplaces/organizations. I have never been accused of taking anything. I was always content with whatever I had.

Another issue to discuss is marital finances. If your partner has an uncontrollable urge to spend more than necessary, it's only a matter of time before you are under financial pressure. And trust me, it's easier for you to act stupid during such a period. Most of the stuff we buy is not even necessary. If you have ever studied the Maslow hierarchy of needs, then you will know how to organize your priorities. But if you can't help your partner to control his/her spending habit, then you have failed in your first task. Partners shape each other - correct and control each other's excesses. If you are not content, you tend to want more. And no matter how much you have, you will always want that latest phone, car, designer clothes, or whatever it may be.

Contentment is a value you should cultivate if you want to maintain your integrity. **DON'T BE GREEDY!!!**

2. DO YOUR DUE DILIGENCE

Be attentive and always conduct thorough research. Don't assume. I know you've heard of stories where somebody was not careful enough, and that caused a great deal of damage. No matter how much effort or time it takes, you must always be diligent.

Something happened to me when I was like 10-11 years old. From that single experience, I was able to figure out early in life what negligence or unfounded assumptions can do to you.

So, I went for this Cadet camp - as we called it then. It was a church thing. I had a small bag that couldn't really contain my stuff, so I had to borrow my late cousin's bigger bag. Although he was much older than me, probably about 15-20 years, he was living with us at that time because of circumstances that I'm not ready to talk about now. It's food for another day. This guy was a player - a serious one. He even had his wife attend one of his girlfriend's (lover's) weddings. I'm not making this stuff up. The innocent woman felt she was attending a friend's wedding, while she didn't realize she was attending her husband's lover's wedding to another man. For us who knew what was really up, we couldn't just wrap our heads around it. We were like, 'When will this guy stop this thing?'

Now let's focus on the real thing. For a 10-year-old who didn't go camping or travel for more than 1-2 days, what kind of big bag would I really have? I mean, will I be going camping for seven days with a really small bag? So, I begged my older cousin for his bag. I'm aware of his reputation with women back then, so I didn't trust him not to have some stuff in his bag. The "innocent me," I don't want to damage my reputation. I searched his bag - this bag had lots of compartments. I couldn't find anything in the major pockets. There were some smaller pockets, and I thought that since I'd been unable to find anything in the other smaller pockets, there wouldn't be anything in these two small pockets. So, I didn't search them.

So, I packed the bag and went to camp with my stuff in the bag. We had lots of fun, but wait for it… things are about to get messy! BOOM!!! One day we were woken up and asked to wait outside while the adult guides searched everyone's bag. Do you know what? Someone stole money while we were sleeping in the night, and since we hadn't had any activities for that day - I mean, it was past 6am, for God's sake, and you can't really prevent something like this in a camp. The counselors, as we called the adult guides back then, figured out that the money would still be in one of the bags in that hostel/dorm. They searched everyone's bag, and then they saw the condoms in one of the pockets that I didn't search. The man who found it was like, what is a 10-year-old doing with a CONDOM?! Imagine the other kids looking at me like, "WOW! That's a really bad child over there." Now there is a bigger problem than the money they were searching for. Well, I had to do a lot of explanation and was eventually recommended for counseling.

Now back to the crux. Due diligence is very important. There are several instances where people have lost their integrity because they failed to take that extra step or do their part diligently, even when someone they know is involved. When it comes to scrutiny, you shouldn't leave anyone out. Just a while ago, I was reading a story on social media. Normally, you have your clique in the office, right? Sometimes we bend the rules for our clique due to the fact that we are acquaintances or friends. There is a problem, though. You're not supposed to do that. A slight mistake can ruin everything you've ever built. There is this story I read recently that backs this up.

A "friend" sneaked into a co-worker's office and used his PC to send a "fake" resignation letter to the management. It took a lot of dialogue and the help of just one person who chose to believe him to save him from this ordeal. Had that person not believed him and stood up for him, he would have been dismissed from his place of work. I'm sure you know that once your resignation letter gets to management, there is no un-doing it. Eventually, the culprit was caught, and he was surprised to see it was his "friend." I mean, they visit each other occasionally, and they roll together after office hours. How did it happen? He left his office open, and seeing his friend along the way, he didn't suspect him one bit, even when he was being questioned about what happened by the HR.

If you go more than a hundred years back to the story of how Germany gained independence from Austria, you will see the effect of diligence in play. I know you may have heard of Von Otto Bismarck and how an Austrian minister signed a very important document without reading the fine print. Yes! The minister gave Germany more than they thought they could get easily. All Bismark needed to do was to upset the minister a little bit such that he did not bother to read the fine print. He felt insulted, and he signed a very important state document in haste. Bismark was very happy because it was a gamble. As for the Austrian minister, I know he would have been very disappointed when he found out eventually.

DO YOUR DUE DILIGENCE.

3. BE DISCIPLINED

It takes a lot of discipline to have integrity. Without discipline, there can be no integrity, and it should be passed down to your children too. If you are not disciplined, you can't be content. Wants are unlimited, and if you are greedy, you will lust over everything. How do you think people will regard you if you are always the one found wanting everything?

4. WHAT ABOUT YOUR CHILDREN?

Parents are praised for their children's good behavior. In Nigeria, and I know it's true for most African countries, the first thing that comes to mind when someone does anything that is extremely bad is that it was passed down from the individual's parents. Bad behavior is not considered random. We so much believe in the influence of parents on their children. Although a lot has changed in our culture, most especially in the region where I come from; however in the old times, if your children wanted to get married, you, as a parent, would investigate the family of the person your child wanted to marry for inheritable diseases, criminal background, etc. It was hard for individuals with a history of crime to get someone to marry them unless they moved out of the community. That's how serious it is. You get backlash for your parents' bad behavior, and parents get backlash for their children's bad behavior.

I'll leave you with a few quotes:

"Real integrity is doing the right thing, knowing that nobody's going to know whether you did it or not." - Unknown

I did some things I'm not proud of in the past; however, I always make amends and never repeat that kind of error again. There you have it.

"**INTEGRITY** - the **INTEGRAL** part of our being." - Unknown

PEACE AND LOVE!

Akinsola Olayinka Oladipupo

If you would like to find out more about Akinsola Olayinka Oladipupo and his services, head to:

https://yinka.gold

ADVANCEMENT

7:

IMAGINATION & CREATIVITY

Advancement 7: Imagination & Creativity

> *"Life is a game. Find the games you want to play, learn the rules and find a way to be SUCCESSFUL."*
>
> *– Kwadw(o) Naya: Baa Ankh Em Re A'lyun Eil*

IMAGINATION and **CREATIVITY** are what makes us individual.

It is true that we are all part of **THE ALL** and **THE ALL** is a part of **US**, meaning that we are **ALL** part of one **UNIVERSAL CONSCIOUSNESS.**

However, **WE ALL** have our part to do.

We are **ALL DIFFERENT** but **EQUAL**.

We are **ALL** part of the **WHOLE**.

Scholars and spiritual teachers throughout history have been proclaiming that there is a state of consciousness of the highest order. They describe it, they characterize it, they paint a picture of it, they point at it, and they suggest that once people enter this enlightened state, they are there. They have arrived! They would have no good reason to leave.

This sounds very good in theory, and **ENLIGHTENMENT** is very good.

But there is **MORE** to **LIFE** than this.

WE ALL need to **PLAY** our **PART**.

WE are **LIKE** the **X-people.**

The **X-men** and **women**, **WE ALL** have our own **POWERS**.

We just need to become **AWARE** of **WHO** and **WHAT WE ARE**.

IMAGINATION and **CREATIVITY** are **KEY**.

YOU SEE, a lot of the **MAGIC** happens when **WE** are in **OUR DREAM STATES**.

Not when **WE** are **BUSY**!

My Grandad used to always say to me:

"Every man has his own strength."

I can only agree with him here.

No two people are the same, not even twins.

Everybody has **IMAGINATION;** everybody can be **CREATIVE** in their own way.

We have all been made in the **IMAGE** of **THE MOST HIGH**, and we are **ALL** connected to **THE SOURCE**.

If **YOU THINK** or **FEEL** different, let me ask you one question?

Where does **YOUR BREATH** come from?

Where does **OUR BREATH** come from?

Please **TELL** me.

Where does **YOUR BREATH** of **LIFE** come from?

Where does **OUR BREATH** of **LIFE** come from?

And what is it connected to?

I am not religious, but I would like to quote a passage from the good old bible as I find it most fitting:

Psalm 82 verse 6:

"I have said, Ye are gods; and all of you are children of the most high."

Apparently, **WE** are All **CHILDREN** of **THE MOST HIGH**, made in the **IMAGE** of **THE MOST HIGH**, meaning that **WE** are **DEITIES OURSELVES**, or should be, through **NATURAL DESCENT**.

If **WE** happen to have **FALLEN** from **GRACE**, that is **OUR OWN BUSINESS**, **WE ALL** should **KNOW** who **WE ARE**.

IMAGINATION and **CREATIVITY** are **VERY IMPORTANT** in **LIFE**.

Without it, there would be no **LIFE**.

Maybe just **STAGNATION**.

We are all **CREATOR GODS**. Well, **MOST** of **US** are. **WE JUST** need to **RE-MEMBER**, **RE-ALIZE**.

Modern religion steers us away from this **MINDSET**.

Advancement 7: Imagination & Creativity

Modern religion teaches and promotes **UTOPIA**.

This sounds good, in theory. But is it?

I am not religious because I like to deal with **FACTS** and **DIVINE TRUTH**.

And religions deal with belief systems.

My father is a bishop, and I must admit I have problems speaking with him now, as he is a **BELIEF DEALER**, whereas I am a **DEALER** in <u>**DIVINE TRUTH**</u> and <u>**UNADULTERATED FACTS**</u>.

I like to either **KNOW** or **NOT KNOW**.

I cannot just **BELIEVE** something because it is the **WAY** that I have been **TAUGHT** or **LED** to **BELIEVE**.

If one **BE-LIE-VES**, they obviously don't **KNOW**. That is all I have to say.

"A belief is a poor substitute for experience." - Tony Robbins

EVIDENCE and **FACTS** are **EVERYTHING**.

Some things are difficult to **QUANTIFY**, but maybe some things are not meant to be **QUANTIFIED**.

Advancement 7: Imagination & Creativity

Let us hear a few words from John Rappaport. He writes a lot on the subjects of **IMAGINATION** and **CREATIVITY** as he **FEELS** that **WE** need to **ALL** tap into **OUR CREATIVE POWERS** in order for us to break out of this **MATRIX** in which most of **US** are **MENTALLY** enslaved.

Let us hear from John:

"Utopia is a deception. It proposes a collective ideal that everyone 'ought to accept' with great joy, but which turns out to be a blunting and shortening of the creative power of every individual.

The creative power of the individual, which is the key to his future, his happiness, his freedom, flows from his imagination."

I actually agree with John in his views in regard to this topic.

Enlightenment is really cool, but it can never be all as you should **KNOW** and **BE AWARE**.

It is ok having humanity all moving or advancing towards **ONENESS, ONE STATE** of **MIND**, and **ONE STATE** of **BEING**.

But this approach is **FLAWED**. Can you not **SEE?**

It could never work without **IMAGINATION** and **CREATIVITY**.

Not **SUCCESSFULLY!**

IMAGINATION and **CREATIVITY** are the **WAY** forward. That is the **PATH** in which the **SUCCESSFUL** travel.

We are all artists with the ability to **CREATE** something out of **NOTHING**.

IDEAS do not **COST MONEY**.

IMAGINATION does not **COST MONEY**.

CREATIVITY never hurt anyone.

The **CREATIVE CONCEPT** is a **MUCH BETTER** approach, obviously.

I LIE?

And **WE** can still adopt those whilst keeping **UTOPIA** with each other.

There should really be no **JEALOUSY** or **REAL** competition as **WE ALL** have **OUR OWN UNIQUE SKILLS** and **POWERS** that we can bring to the **WORLD TABLE**.

We **ALL HAVE OUR PART** to **PLAY** in the **GRAND SCHEME** of **THINGS** – **KNOW THIS!**

What are **YOUR THOUGHTS** on **ALL** of **THIS?**

As I was saying, **WE** are **CREATORS**.

WE are the **CREATOR GODS** and **GODDESSES**.

WE ARE ARTISTS.

WE have **IMAGINATION.**

The **STATES** of **OUR OWN INDIVIDUAL CONSCIOUSNESS** become our own inventions.

WE PAINT WHATEVER PICTURE that **WE WANT** with **OUR IMAGINATIONS** and **IMPLEMENT** it with **OUR CREATIVITY.**

To us anything is **POSSIBLE** as we are the **CREATOR GODS** and **GODDESSES**. We can envisage and **CREATE** without limitations. We just need to **FIND OUR OWN UNIQUE POWERS** and **PURPOSE.**

Everything **WE SEE** is a **RESULT** of a **PICTURE** (that was once) in someone's **MIND.**

Please do not forget this.

There is nothing in the nature of consciousness that implies all individuals' choices should arrive at the same destination. This would make no sense at all.

We are not saying that people should not get on. We are **SAYING** that people should not forget themselves. They should not forget who and what they really are.

Are you with me?

In one previous book I wrote, I was referring to **CHOICES**. One choice we all need to make is whether **WE** are going to take the natural route to life or the unnatural.

THAT CHOICE is yours.

I FEEL that <u>IMAGINATION</u> and <u>CREATIVITY</u> should be ENCOURAGED throughout the world. It is only then that the world can be in the place that it should be.

Where it needs to be.

Did **YOU KNOW THAT THIS PLAN-E.T.** is a **LIVING ENTITY?**

It is **TRUE**. That is **WHY WE ALL** have a **RESPONSIBILITY** to **LOOK** after **HER. OTHERWISE, SHE WILL** not

LOOK AFTER US.

And just **FACE** it, **WHATEVER HAPPENS TO US – SHE DECIDES!**

!!! BE CAREFUL !!!

When **ALL** individuals are tapping into their **CREATIVE CAPACITIES** with **IMAGINATION** and **DIVINE LOVE**, they are **SERVING** their **PURPOSE**, **EACH** doing their **OWN UNIQUE** part for **HUMANITY**.

I **SEE** this as the **ONLY TRUE WORKABLE** situation for **OUR HUMANITY**.

And if this was the case, we would truly see an open society in which individuals **CREATE** and **INVENT** many realities as opposed to everybody somehow arriving at a single "utopia."

What do you **THINK** about **ALL** of **THIS?**

PEACE AND LOVE!

Kwadw(o) Naya: Baa Ankh Em Re A'lyun Eil

If you would like to find out more about Kwadw(o) Naya: Baa

Advancement 7: Imagination & Creativity

Ankh Em Re A'lyun Eil and his services, head to:

https://kwadwonayabaaankhemrealyuneil.gold/

ADVANCEMENT

WHO IS GOD & THE DEVIL?

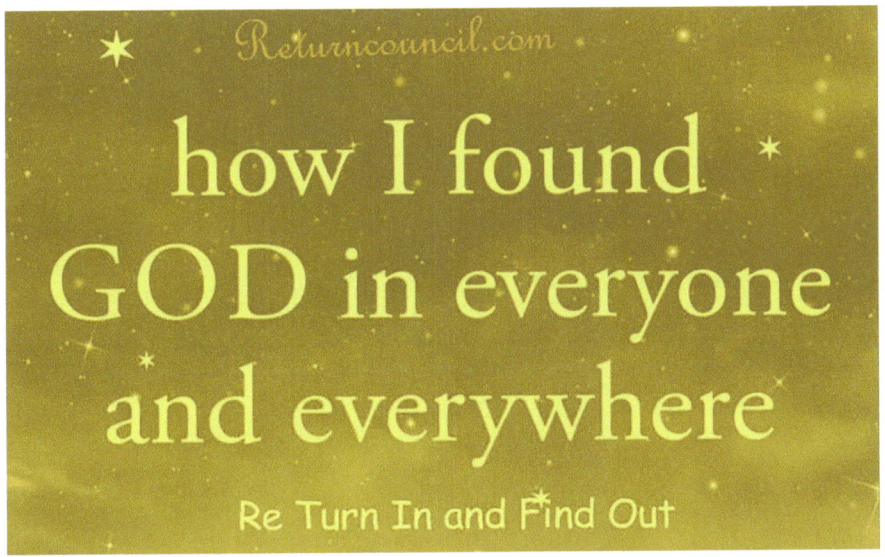

WHO IS GOD AND THE DEVIL?

ANSWER: Remember what humans assumed **WHAT GOD** was and is your higher self that is why **GOD** appeared to religious people it's really you your higher self your soul your spirit your over soul that is why some preachers say **GOD** spoke to them last night and say so and so.

It was you all along that was and is **THE MOST HIGH GOD.**

And as you pretend not to be in contact with this **MOST HIGH GOD** (which is yourself), you created a longing to connect with your higher self, your soul, and your **OVERSOUL**, you created fear, and that fear caused us to create a most high God outside ourselves.

And your **INNER ME** "enemy" is your favorite nemesis, the devil.

It's all a joke from the third dimension.

It has no validity in **5D**.

That is, in a nutshell. All of you are **NUTS** in a shell called the human body. You are **NUTS** searching for yourself. Research **HU NUT** is.

WELCOME to the **RE-TURN!**

As you are counseled and re-minded by memo from **RE** "memory".

A **RE**-minder from the mind of **RE**.

Amun Harkhuf **TEHUTI** of the order of **EGYPT**,

SAYF of the ancient mystical order of Melchizedek,

Dr. Shawn Pereira of The Holy Tabernacle Ministries,

and A Yanuwnite from the 8th planet Rizq "marzaq".

The Re-turn Council

A council of **AMUN RAYAY.**

PEACE AND LOVE!

Shawn Pereira

You can find out more about Shawn and how he can help and assist by visiting his website:

https://www.returncouncil.com

ADVANCEMENT

THE RAPTURE IS HERE & NOW!

Advancement 9: The Rapture Is Here & Now

Many people have an **IDEA** of **THE RAPTURE**.

Many people **DO NOT**.

So…

What is **THE RAPTURE?**

GOOD QUESTION 😊.

Let us first have a **LOOK** at the **DEFINITIONS:**

rapture

/ˈraptʃə/

noun

1. a feeling of intense pleasure or joy.

1. "Leonora listened with rapture."

NORTH AMERICAN

According to millenarian teaching, the transporting of believers to heaven at the Second Coming of Christ.

"Thousands of Christians gathered outside Rochester and other cities, awaiting the Rapture."

verb

NORTH AMERICAN

According to millenarian teaching, transport (a believer) from earth to heaven at the Second Coming of Christ.

"People will be raptured out of automobiles as they are driving along."

Similar words: ecstasy, bliss, euphoria, elation, exaltation, joy, joyfulness, joyousness, cloud nine, seventh heaven, transport, rhapsody, enchantment, delight, exhilaration, happiness, pleasure, ravishment, the top of the world, delectation.

Opposite words: boredom, indifference.

https://languages.oup.com/google-dictionary-en/ accessed 8th January 2021 @ 12:26

Let us also **SEE** what good 'ole' Wikipedia is saying:

The rapture is an eschatological theological position held by some Christians, particularly within branches of American evangelicalism, consisting of an end-time event when all Christian believers who are alive, along with resurrected believers, would rise in the clouds, to meet the Lord in the air.

So.

What's up with **THE RAPTURE?**

GOOD QUESTION 😊

<u>THE RAPTURE IS HERE AND NOW!</u>

In the scriptures, when they talk about a rapture, they're talking about an elevation of consciousness.

An expansion of consciousness.

Those who are rising above the perceived and acknowledged level of perception that most people have, with rapture.

Elevating beyond the below-normal level of consciousness where most people are.

And I say below the normal level of consciousness because your normal level of consciousness is **ETERNITY**.

The below-normal level of consciousness is mortality.

Those who reach what has become also **KNOWN** as **THE CHRIST CONSCIOUSNESS!**

THE GOD CONSCIOUSNESS!

ENLIGHTENED!

Have tapped into **THE ETERNAL!**

Many of us are trapped in our normal levels, or should I say "our normal levels below that." So we're only dealing with a **3D STATE** of persons, places, and things.

YOU bel-lie-ve yourself to be simply **THIS BODY, YOUR EMOTIONS, YOUR THOUGHTS, YOUR SENSATIONS.**

And all of that is **EXPERIENCED THROUGH YOUR BODY.**

YOUR CAR.

YOUR body, **YOUR** car, **YOUR** spirit, and **YOUR SOUL!**

YOUR EMOTIONAL BODY, through **YOUR SENSES:**

- Touch
- Taste
- Smell
- Feel
- Hear
- See

Those who <u>**DO NOT EXPAND**</u> to the normal levels of **CONSCIOUSNESS**, which is **ETERNITY.**

THE OMNIPRESENT SELF IS LEFT BEHIND.

It is happening right now.

LOOK AROUND. If **YOU OBSERVE** and **YOU** are **AWARE, YOU WILL SEE,** for **SURE!**

But sadly, these days, too many of **US** are **SUFFERING** from **AMNESIA** caused historically by **EVIL INCANTATIONS** and **SPELLS** of **SLEEP** and **IGNORANCE.**

THINGS ARE CHANGING – RIGHT NOW!

To be honest with **YOU,** I do not **KNOW** what is going to happen to those who do not reach their normal level of consciousness.

YES, I DO KNOW!

THEY WILL PERISH!

OR YOU WILL JUST COMPLETE THE SAME EARTH SCHOOL ONCE YOUR BODY DIES, THEN, AS A FRAGMENT OR A PART OF OR AS AN INDIVIDUAL SPIRIT, YOU WILL HAVE TO COME BACK HERE AND DO IT AGAIN.

To come and do this earth experience again.

Many people are simply satisfied with the **conditioned MIND.**

We just want to live, marry, intermingle, have fun, have sex and eat, go to exotic places and eventually die.

Most people have the limited perception that "I'm gonna have all my fun now, and then when I get old, I'll slow down and maybe go fishing or something, find a new hobby, retire."

That perceived way of living is delusional. You can have **ETERNITY** right here, right now.

One of the scriptures said, "Jesus said the works that I do, **YOU'LL DO GREATER!**"

MY QUESTION TO ALL YOU CHRISTIANS IS, HOW CAN YOU DO GREATER WORKS IN CHRIST?

Some of God's works include <u>**RAISING THE DEAD**</u> and <u>**GIVIVG SIGHT**</u> to **THE BLIND**.

So, for those who can't **SEE BEYOND** or can't **EXPOUND**, **KINDLY TELL ME <u>HOW</u> ARE YOU GOING TO DO GREATER THAN HIM???**

IF YOU CLAIM TO BE A CHRISTIAN, <u>HOW ARE YOU GOING TO DO GREATER</u>?

HOW CAN YOU DO THE SAME?

First, **YOU** have got to **FIGURE OUT HOW TO DO** the same.

There is **ONLY ONE WAY!**

YOU HAVE TO SHIFT YOUR LEVEL OF CONSCIOUSNESS.

In <u>**the scriptures,**</u> they say:

"Two people will be laying in the bed or two people on the field, and one is going to leave the other behind."

THAT is happening – **RIGHT NOW!**

<u>**EVERYTHING IS RIGHT NOW**</u>**!**

TIME is either a **MEMORY** or **PROJECTION,** which gives **YOU YOUR PAST** and **FUTURE,** or is based on the **ROTATION** of **THE PLANET** on its axis and around <u>**THE SUN**</u>**.**

This is man-made.

That part, I mean **THE PLANET ROTATING AROUND THE SUN,** and on its axis, is **NATURE.**

<u>**IT'S DIVINE!**</u>

BUT CLOCKING IT AND GIVING IT 365 DAYS A YEAR AND ALL THAT AND SAYING THIS IS THIS TIME AND THAT TIME, that's all down to man.

Advancement 9: The Rapture Is Here & Now

And the most delusional concept of **TIME** is **PSYCHOLOGICAL.**

Most people are **TRAPPED** in that **PSYCHOLOGICAL TIME WARP,** which makes it **DELUSIONAL.**

YOUR people are **TRAPPED IN THEIR PAST.**

YOU KNOW – IN THEIR MEMORY.

They are <u>**JUDGING**</u> this, <u>**THEIR MOMENT, THEIR REALITY.**</u>

<u>**THEY'RE JUDGING NOW!**</u>

<u>**OR STUCK IN A TIME OF THE PAST – JUDGING IT AND APPLYING IT TO NOW!**</u>

INSTEAD OF EXPERIENCING THE BEAUTY OF NOW - THE SPONTANEOUS – THE UNKNOWN, THE EXCITEMENT OF NOW, THE BEWILDERMENT OF NOW.

I don't **KNOW** what is going to happen next, but I am **FULLY EMBRACING THE OMNIPRESENT SELF, EVER READY TO RESPOND** to whatever happens in **'THE MOMENT.'**

That is the **JOY** of **LIFE!**

YOU COULD DROP DEAD RIGHT NOW.

And people are dropping dead **RIGHT NOW!**

LOVED ONES.

There is that **STATE** of **ETERNITY** that has **NO BEGINNING** nor **NO END,** and **YOU** can **DISCOVER** this **RIGHT NOW.**

WE ARE HERE TO HELP YOU REACH THAT LEVEL OF CONSCIOUSNESS!

But **YOU** have got to **WANT** it.

And **YOU have** got to **ASK for it!**

If **YOU DON'T ASK** for it, then **YOU'RE NOT** going to **OPEN YOURSELF UP** – to **BE RAISED** or **RESURRECTED** from **THE DEAD.**

THE MENTALLY DEAD – WE ARE NOT GOING TO BE ABLE TO HELP YOU!

It is a **GRADUAL PROCESS** for a lot of people – in **FACT,** it is for **ALL OF US!**

I didn't just reach this level instantly, although one could make an argument to say that it has been instantly if **NOW IS ALWAYS THE TIME**!

And **NOW IS ALWAYS THE TIME**!

It's just a matter of **US CATCHING UP TO IT**!

Redirecting our attention to it.

Becoming **AWARE** of it.

And **ALIGNING OURSELVES** with it.

That's also called **GRACE**!

I refuse at this point in **THIS JOURNEY to WATER ANYTHING DOWN.**

That is why I am having a hard time fitting in with a lot of people's reality or unreality.

I can get along, and I can move along with others for a little while but not long because it is **TIME** for the **WHOLE TRUTH** and **NOTHING BUT THE TRUTH**!

There is **NO SENSE** in even **PLAYING AROUND** with **ANYTHING** less than that.

Advancement 9: The Rapture Is Here & Now

IS THERE?

WHAT WOULD BE THE POINT?

I RESPECT EVERYBODY'S LEVEL OF CONSCIOUSNESS.

<u>YOU ARE WHO YOU ARE</u>!

And I hope wherever **YOU** are that **YOU'RE** doing <u>**POSITIVE WORKS**</u> because that <u>**MATTERS**</u>.

Those who are putting in **GOOD WORKS INHERIT A <u>PIECE OF HEAVEN</u>**.

Those doing **NEGATIVE WORKS** will inherit a **PIECE** of <u>**HELL!**</u>

Some of **US** carrying out <u>**POSITIVE WORKS**</u> are still **EXPERIENCING HELL** because **HELL** is just a lower <u>**VIBRATION**</u> that <u>**CREATES SUFFERING**</u>!

This is it for now.

It has been a pleasure spending this **TIME** with **YOU**. I **LOOK** forward to catching up with **YOU** in **The Raising of The 144,000 – Scroll 2.**

PEACE AND LOVE!

Dr. Leon Moss (Aka Hotep Tal Amun)

Feel free to visit my website, look around, check out the services, etc. We are always here to help:

https://www.drleonmoss.gold/

CONCLUSION

Conclusion

I would firstly like to thank all of you wonderful readers for purchasing and reading this scroll, without **YOU** this book would have no purpose. So **THANK YOU** from **ME** and **EVERYONE ELSE** at **GOLDEN CHILD PROMOTIONS PUBLISHING.**

Secondly, I would like to take this time to thank all of the authors that have participated in the **CREATION** of this book, I greatly enjoyed reading through the chapters in suspense of this conclusion to be written.

Firstly I must say that we have collectively done a **DIVINE** thing.

This **DIVINE** thing is **CREATION.**

Now you as the reader may agree or disagree with its contents, but the fact of **CREATION** being a **DIVINE** property is **IRREFUTABLE.** We are simply attempting to **ENLIGHTEN** you with our observations, with no responsibility for the outcome, one man or woman sows another man or woman reaps. Those with eyes to see, let them see and those with ears to hear let them hear.

I didn't create your eyes or ears and I didn't separate the wheat from the chaff. I am just here to deliver the message to those willing souls that are opened and attuned to the frequency.

This is the holy **SPIRIT** that lives in us if we choose to accept it. This **SPIRIT** connects all those with it to each other in the realm of **CREATIVITITY, LOVE, PEACE** and **JOY** etc... The **FRUITS** of the **SPIRIT** are made flesh through the process of faith in **THE MOST HIGH GOD!**

DO YOU SEE?

There is nothing on this earth with the value of wisdom. Wisdom is more valuable than Gold. I would rather be rich in wisdom but poor in gold than rich in gold but poor in wisdom.

WOULDN'T YOU?

This question you'd think to be a no-brainer but that's exactly the methodology that the majority use. "**NO BRAIN**... er..." **(NO THOUGHTS), AND** then they choose the **GOLD... (DUH).**

I'd imagine if you made it this far through the book you are not one of those people. Who am I to assume this, however?

Maybe you have great tenacity to endure the great suffering in regards to entertaining these bunch of crazies, but I again assume that you didn't and that you enjoyed your time reading the first scroll from the **"Raising of the 144,000"** with us at Golden Child Promotions Publishing.

MAYBE you are one of the 144,000 too?

What do you **THINK?**

Have you always **FELT DIFFERENT?**

ALIEN even?

As if you are **IN THIS WORLD** but **NOT FROM IT?**

This is common within the world of **TRUTH SEEKING** yet uncommon for those still stuck in their **3D** reality completely entertained by the objects of the world. If you feel alien. I hope you felt some camaraderie and sense of likeness of thought whilst indulging in these pages.

We are intending to publish the second **"Raising of the 144,000"** scroll soon, and hope to see you back there for scroll 2. If you have any comments relating to any of the chapters or would like to know more, feel free to contact any of the authors. You will find the link to each author's website at the end of each chapter. Finally, feel free to check out Golden Child Promotions Publishing which is our hub for knowledge, wisdom, and reaching our highest frequency.

Conclusion

https://goldenchildpromotionspublishing.gold

Once again thank you for reading this. May God gift you with the peace that surpasses all understanding, signing out: - **Daniel Owen Raine**

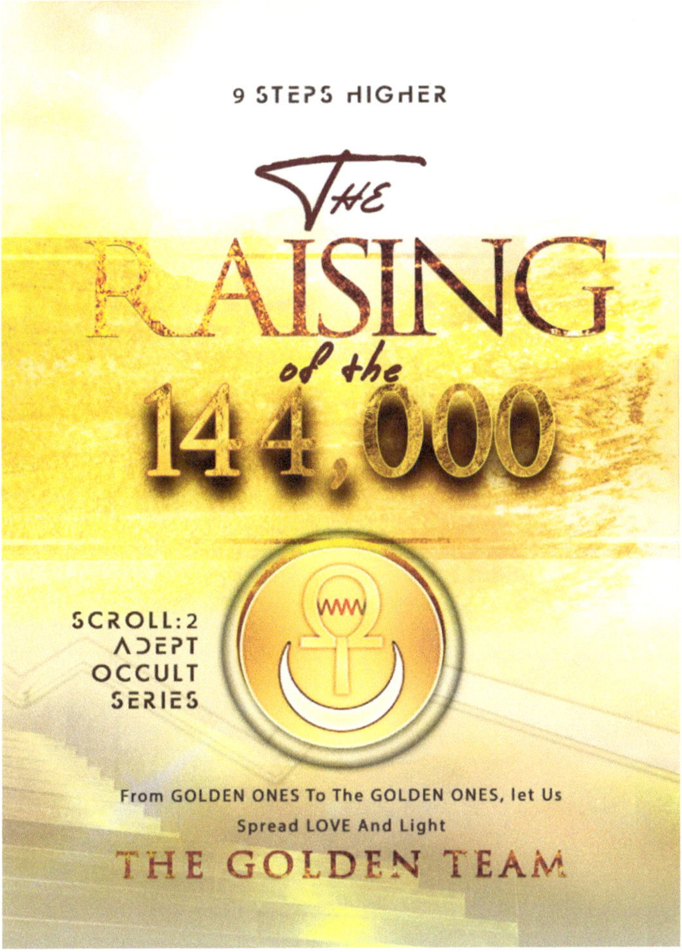
9 STEPS HIGHER
THE
RAISING
of the
144,000
SCROLL:2
ADEPT
OCCULT
SERIES
From GOLDEN ONES To The GOLDEN ONES, let Us
Spread LOVE And Light
THE GOLDEN TEAM

COMING SOON!

AFTERWORD

Afterword

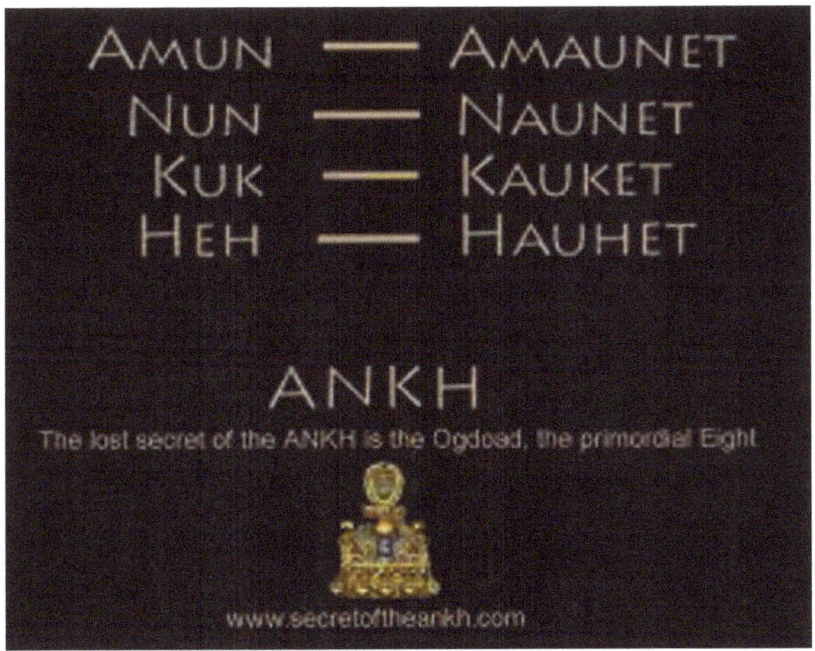

We spoke about **THE ANKH** during the preface of this book.

We broke it down a little but didn't quite finish off.

As you may **KNOW** or **NOT**, the **ANKH** is one of the **KEYS** to **LIFE**.

When **YOU** get **CHANCE**, **LOOK** into **THE ANKH**.

DO YOUR OWN RESEARCH, do not just **TAKE** what **WE SAY AS FACT**, without **CHECKING THINGS PROPERLY YOURSELF.**

Afterword

LOOK into **THE WORD A.N.K.H.**

SEE WHAT IT REPRESENTS AND STANDS FOR.

SEE WHO:

A-mun/Amunet

N-un/Nunet

K-ek/Kekhet

H-eh/Hehet

ARE and **WHAT POWERS** that they **BRING FORTH.**

LOOK at how the **WHOLE** of this **PLAN-E.T.** has been **PUT TOGETHER.**

We spoke a little about **AMUN** and **AMUNET** during the preface section of this book but we didn't **LOOK** into **KEK** and **KEKHET** or **HEH** or **HEHET.**

The Ogdoad consisted of four pairs of deities, four male gods paired with their female counterparts.

KEK and **KEKHET** are the ancient Egyptian deities of night and darkness.

Kek (mythology) - Wikipedia

Kekui

Accessed 24th October 2022 @ 16:08

HEH or **HEHET** represent **ETERNITY,** somewhere that happens to be **OUTSIDE** the **REALM** of **TIME.**

Ogdoad, Deir el Medina, SFE Cameron, via Wikimedia Commons - accessed 24th October 2022 @ 16:22

Check out the next extract:

"The Ogdoad was a system of eight deities, four gods and their consorts (the number four was considered to represent

Afterword

completeness). Each pair represented the male and female aspects of the four creative powers or sources. Nun and Naunet represented the primeval waters; Heh and Hauhet represented eternity; Kuk and Kauket represented darkness; and Amun and Amunet represented air (or that which is hidden). However, the gods differ from one source to another." https://ancientegyptonline.co.uk/ogdoad/ accessed 24th October 2022 @ 16:22

As **YOU** can **SEE** from **LOOKING** at **THE BIG PICTURE, THE A.N.K.H.** encodes not only **THE MEANING OF LIFE**, and **THE POWERS** but **THE CREATION OF LIFE ITSELF.**

DO YOU OVER-stand?

When you get **CHANCE LOOK** into the **STORY** about the **OGDOAD** and the **9 ENNEADS**.

Afterword

I hope you enjoyed this book, it has been a **GREAT PLEASURE** as **ALWAYS.**

Hopefully we will see **YOU** in the next **INSTALMENT** of The Raising of The 144,000 which will be **REALEASED APRIL 2023.**

PEACE & LOVE

Kwadw(o) Naya: Baa A.n.k.h. Em Re A'lyun Eil

https://kwadwonayabaaankhemrealyuneil.gold/

ABOUT THE AUTHORS

About The Authors

DR. LEON MOSS

I Am as I Am, also known as Dr. Leon Moss and spiritually known as Hotep Talah Amun, is an author, businessman, and spiritual guide. Dr. Leon Moss attended the University of the Holy Tabernacle Ministries in 1993 and received a Doctorate of Divinity in the field of theology, history, comparative religious studies, and Semitic languages. Dr. Leon Moss is a High Priest after the Order of Melchizedek and an eternal member of the ancient Egyptian order.

About The Authors

If you would like to like to find out more about Dr. Leon Moss, his books, services, video logs, how he can help you, etc., you can visit his website:

https://www.drleonmoss.gold

KWADW(O) NAYA: BAA ANKH EM RE A'LYUN EIL

Some call him Kwadw(o), others call him Baa. He is a successful author, life coach, mentor, businessman and founder of Golden Child Promotions Publishing Ltd. After a turbulent childhood, and losing his business on his 40th birthday, Kwadw(o) Naya: Baa Ankh Em Re A'lyun Eil is a beacon of inspiration and a testament to what can happen if you let go and trust the Universe to guide you to your purpose. Kwadw(o) went from losing everything to doing something he never thought he could do: write. Today, Baa has written and published over 40 books, and his organisation is dedicated to sharing his vision, values, and wisdom with others who want a new start in life. To find out more about Kwad(o) and how to work with him visit:

https://kwadwonayabaaankhemrealyuneil.gold/

SHAWN PEREIRA: AKA SYLVESTER LLEWELLYN

Shawn Pereira is the founder of the Return Council Omniversity, a self-help school to help souls remember who they were before their incarnation. Shawn is also a certified counselor and a member of the Ancient Egyptian Order and the Ancient and Mystical Order of Melchisedek. He wants to help people raise their vibrations and expand their awareness as cosmic citizens.

About The Authors

You can find out more about Shawn and how he can help and assist by visiting his website:

https://www.returncouncil.com

DANIEL OWEN RAINE

The name, Daniel Owen Raine, translates to Daniel (God is my judge), Owen (Young Warrior), and Raine (Wise Ruler). Daniel's first worldly love was computers, and he became a software engineer. As a result of constantly sitting at a desk, Daniel developed poor posture and started a mission to learn about the body, which led him to personal training. Alongside his commercial work, Daniel has been teaching through speech and videos, writing about life, and leading others to become the best version of themselves which leads him to attribute himself as an author, mentor, and coach.

Daniel's mother committed suicide when he was six years old, which was a catalyst for all of the titles that he has since collected. God's plan is good, and the events, both positive and negative, have led Daniel to this moment here, so for that, he has nothing but joy and gratitude.

If you would like to find out more about Daniel Owen Raine and his services, head to:

https://danielowenraine.gold

CYRLENE

I'm so pleased and privileged to have been given this opportunity to be amongst other experienced authors. I was once told at university that I write in a journalistic way. I was really surprised the way I expressed myself was put in this box, so it knocked my confidence. I was overthinking and came to the conclusion that we can write and express ourselves in any way we please because it's coming from us.

I know I'm expected to write it in the third person, but I think it makes sense to talk directly to you, the audience who are going to be reading about me in this book... you guessed it - I'm here to break all the rules and reach my tribe the way I would like to.

My chapter touches on some of the traumas I have experienced throughout my life. I plan to expand on each story in the future. I hope to build my fan base of women that can relate to some of the issues I have experienced and then bring some of these topics into the open through discussions and workshops.

Feel free to visit my website and see how I can help you to **EMPOWER YOUR – SELF.**

https://cyrlene.gold.

About The Authors

AKINSOLA OLAYINKA OLADIPUPO

Akinsola Olayinka Oladipupo is the Creative Director and Campaign Coordinator for Golden Child Promotions Publishing Ltd. He is a graphic designer from Nigeria with a special interest in print design, ebook design, web design, and branding for book authors. Akinsola has worked with small businesses and large global conglomerates for several years.

As a strong believer in '**KAIZEN**,' Akinsola is always building a better version of himself through seeking new knowledge; and as a new author, he uses his writing style to help people build the character needed to form a formidable and better version of themselves too.

If you would like to find out more about Akinsola Olayinka Oladipupo and his services, head to:

https://yinka.gold.

"1 + 4 + 4 = 9 ether"

- Dr Leon Moss

www.ingramcontent.com/pod-product-compliance
Lightning Source LLC
Chambersburg PA
CBHW040159100526
44590CB00001B/3